SECOND EDITION

THE GULLAH PEOPLE

OF SANDY ISLAND

0-9767079-1-8

A Tribute to The Gullah People Of Sandy Island, S.C.

Dedication

This book is dedicated to the Gullah people of Sandy Island, S.C. A special dedication posthumously to my parents, Charlie Sr. and Sarah G. Pyatt. My father was born and raised on Sandy Island. Sandy Island has remained mostly unchanged for centuries. The proud and strong Gullah people on Sandy Island today are direct descendants of the great Gullah people who were involuntarily brought to these shores centuries ago.

The Gullah people on Sandy Island have given me such great inspiration to remain proud and strong and to push on when things seem bleak. I can remember my early years when I spent the summers on Sandy Island and was amazed at the independence of the Gullah people of Sandy Island. I still get strength and courage from visiting my relatives on the island, especially my uncle Samuel who still resides in Annie Village (his childhood home) on Sandy Island.

A Special Tribute to Mom and Dad With Deep Appreciation and Gratitude

It has often been said that if one forgets his history, he is condemned to repeat it. A person must have the knowledge of who they are, a knowledge of self. Otherwise they will very easily get caught up in the snares of the world. Always remember your rich culture and heritage. It is often the parents who make the greatest impression on their children at a very young age. Mom and Dad provided for us from day one. They started out with a small apartment in Tin Top Alley. They worked hard and provided for us and saved enough to build a house a few blocks away that stands to this day. They had three children and two more would be born in the new house.

It must have been very difficult in those days, but they were very strong God fearing people with a deep faith and sense of self worth. They provided sufficient food and shelter, and gave us a very profound upbringing with a strong foundation in God.

They had such Wisdom, Knowledge and Understanding that could have only come from God. They were both forced to go to work at a very young age because one of their parents had died. They had the experience of life, and instilled in us what we needed to excel in this wayfaring land.

When they first moved to their new house from the apartment in Tin Top Alley, the road was not paved and got muddy when it rained. In those days it was the other side of town. They protected us from terror in the night and endured and overcame many obstacles. Their struggles and sacrifices made it possible for us to enjoy the good life today. I'm sure this contributed to our success today. We can see it in what we have accomplished and obtained, based on the foundation they instilled in us. They made it possible for us to get a very good education and enjoy what we have today. We must never forget their history, for it is our history. We are what we are today because of their sacrifices and guidance. They did not have or enjoyed some of the material things we have today. But their life was filled with a deep and abiding faith that brought them through in better shape than many of the youngsters of today.

The house they built stills stands today, and is a memorial and living legacy to them. It was a joy growing up in that house in a community with a deep sense of caring, and with good neighbors. A far cry from the drive by, TV generation of today, where many are hooked on untold mind twisters and other folly.

Mom and Dad you were and are so special, a tribute is not sufficient. Our Appreciation and Gratitude is Eternal, and we thank God for letting you do what you did for us. Placing a flower is but a small token of our appreciation and deep respect. We know that we shall meet again, even beyond that great millennium. As all God's children will be with Him in that Great Eternity. Thank God for Mom and Dad.
Amen.

Thomas J. Pyatt

Contents

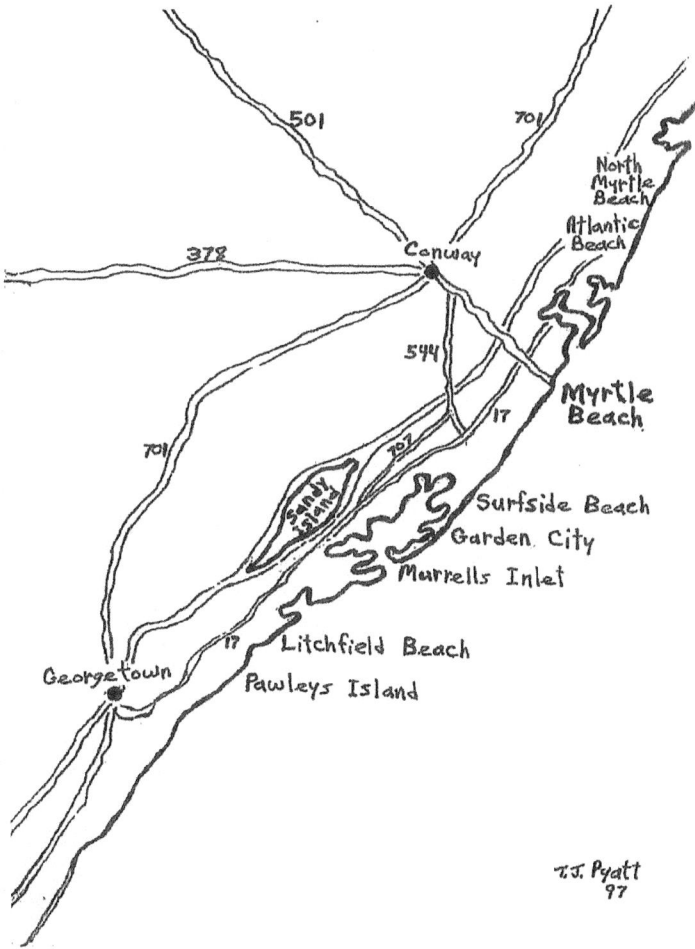

501

701

North Myrtle Beach

378

Conway

Atlantic Beach

544

Myrtle Beach

17

701

707

Sandy Island

Surfside Beach

Garden City

Murrells Inlet

17

Litchfield Beach

Georgetown

Pawleys Island

T.J. Pyatt 97

vii

701

Sandy
Island

Annie
Village

Mt.
Arena

Great Pee Dee River

Waccamaw River

17

Introduction

The Gullah-Geechee culture is unique to the coastal areas and sea islands of the Carolinas, Georgia and Florida. It is known as Gullah in the Carolinas and as Geechee in Florida and Georgia. The Gullah-Geechee people are direct descendants of residents of West Africa's rice coast who were brought here as slaves to work the fertile coastal areas. When the captains of slave ships brought Africans to America, they dropped many of their captives off at Charleston, S.C. which was America's largest slave marketing center in the 18th century. It has been estimated that over one third of Blacks can trace their history to the Charleston seaport.

Many of the slaves were taken to plantations on the isolated barrier islands off the South Carolina coast. Many of the plantations were rice plantations along the waccamaw neck along the Waccamaw River. And even though stripped of their homeland and forced to live in isolated patches they continued to speak their language and retain their culture. The Gullah culture, handed down by West African slaves, is still alive on Sandy Island and the island communities along the South Carolina coast. For over 300 years the Gullah people have resided in these low lying isolated pockets. The lack of bridges to the islands left the Gullah culture unspoiled and pristine with its dominant motherland influences. The isolation retained their distinct cultural differences from mainland residents.

The Gullah people of today that reside on Sandy Island are direct descendants of the Gullah people who were brought here centuries ago. The Gullah people of today have maintained an ongoing fight to preserve their culture as handed down to them from their ancestors, as the culture has been handed down from generation to generation, and has a major impact on how they function as a group of people. Sandy Island is still pretty much isolated as there are no bridges to the island, and electricity didn't come to the Island until about 1967 and running water didn't come until 2001.

SANDY ISLAND

Sandy Island is located about three miles west of the Atlantic Ocean, and is surrounded by the Waccamaw River on the East, the Great Pee Dee River on the West, Bull Creek on the North, and Thoroughfare Creek on the South. Sandy Island is about 30 miles southwest of Myrtle Beach, S.C.

In the early 1800's the wetlands of Sandy Island were converted to rice fields along the Waccamaw River. There were a number of plantations along the Waccamaw River, such as, Pipe Down, Taylor Hill, Blain, Laurel Hill, The Oaks, Oak Lawn, Oak Hampton, Sandy Knowe and Ruinsville. This area had the second largest rice culture in history (China had largest). The rice was called "Waccamaw Gold" and was exported to Europe, etc.

The residents of West Africa were expert rice producers and farmers and were involuntarily brought to these shores to work the rice plantations as slaves. With the cheap labor it was easy to make the price of the rice competitive and large profits were made for the wealthy plantation owners. The low-country area was ideally suited for growing rice with its fertile land, and the West Africans were expert rice producers.

The residents of Sandy Island today are direct descendants of the Gullah people. The names are the same, such as, the Pyatt's, Herriott, Washington, Elliott, Lance, Tucker, Weathers, Deas, etc. The history of the island and people were passed down from generation to generation. My uncle Samuel told me about his grandfather Nehemiah and how it was like for the older generations growing up on the island. They made the best of some difficult times and their fortitude carried them through some very difficult situations.

The Sandy Island Preserve

Sandy Island is one of the last remaining islands that have not fallen to development by big developers. There have been attempts over the years by developers to develop Sandy Island, and the last attempt failed in 1996. Sandy Island is a 12,000 acre island with unique wetlands, wildlife, plants and centuries old moss trees. The state of South Carolina now owns most of the island and less than 25% of the island is now privately owned. The state of South Carolina realized that most of the island should be preserved in its natural setting and the wetlands preserved forever. The South Carolina Department of Transportation (SCDOT) purchased over 9,000 acres on the island to preserve it forever for the people of South Carolina and all people who cherishes keeping some things the way they were centuries ago in their natural and pristine setting.

The state retained the Nature Conservancy (a nonprofit group) to manage the island. This insures that the wetlands, marshes and forests will be protected. And also so that wildfires will be better prevented, contained and controlled before destroying untold acres of the natural beauty and pristine settings of the island. Cookouts are not allowed on the public portion of the island and neither are motorized vehicles or bicycles. There are no guided tours or public facilities on the island, and visitors should remain on the main trails unless accompanied by locals or someone who knows the island. Many parts of the island are extremely isolated and you must know where you are going when you venture from the main trails.

There are no bridges to the 12,000 acre island, and the island has been isolated and undeveloped for centuries. There are no stores on the island and the trails and sandy roads are unimproved. Wildlife is abundant including some rare species along with the snakes and alligators. The inhabitants of the island seem happy with their way of life and look forward to keeping the island in its isolated and natural setting.

Gullah Settlements on Sandy Island

There are three settlements on Sandy Island today in which the Gullah People reside, Mt. Arena, Annie Village and Georgia Hill. Other private landowners reside in some of the other areas and there are also hunting lodges and cabins on part of the island. The Gullah settlements are located on the southeastern portion of the island. Annie Village is about two miles north of Mt. Arena and Georgia Hill is about two hundred yards north of Annie Village.

Mt. Arena is the largest Gullah settlement on Sandy Island and is the focal point of the Gullah people on the island. The old school is located at Mt. Arena although it is not in use anymore, and would be ideally suited for a community center and a cultural and heritage center. A playground for the children is located at Mt. Arena and the church is located not too far away. A large boat dock is at Mt. Arena where the Gullah people from all three settlements dock their boats when they arrive on Sandy Island after crossing the Waccamaw River from the Sandy Island Landing at the mainland.

They must leave their cars parked at the Sandy Island Landing, and this is where the school bus picks up the children to carry them to schools farther on the mainland. Once the Gullah people get to the boat dock at Mt. Arena they must then walk or ride in one of the few vehicles to get to their houses at Mt. Arena or one of the other two Gullah settlements on the island. Other private landowners have their own boat docks at their private estates a little further south of Mt. Arena.

Mt. Arena is the gathering place for a number of Gullah events and is used for some reunion events, cookouts, picnics and get-togethers. Mt. Arena and the surrounding area contain a number of artifacts and have always been historically significant. Mt. Arena is where the first group of about thirty freed slave families settled and built their homes and church.

The riverbank at Mt. Arena has been a special place for each generation and stories have been passed down about various events that have occurred there. The boat dock is like a gathering place especially in the morning when the residents arrive at about the same time to go to work or school on the mainland. It's a place to see people and socialize a bit before the long day begins.

At the riverbank you can watch the tide come in at high tide and see it go out at low tide. At low tide you can see the Skelton of the old school boat as it sits on the mud bottom of the river so close to shore. The Gullah people who reside at Mt. Arena today are direct descendants of those first settlers of Mt. Arena.

Right there beside the bank of the Waccamaw River reside the great, great, great grands, and the great, great, great, great grands. There are also a few great, great, great, great, great grands that are fairly young.

The Gullah People of Sandy Island

Sandy Island has a very deep and rich history as it relates to the Gullah people. In the early days there were nine rice plantations along the Waccamaw River, and the Gullah people produced some of the best rice in the world. But this only benefited the wealthy rice planters who exported the rice (Waccamaw Gold). During post reconstruction, a former slave, Phillip Washington, amassed enough money to buy 382 acres of land in 1882 from Eliza Herriott the widow of a plantation owner. My aunt Francis Herriott Pyatt was the great great granddaughter of Phillip Washington.

During post reconstruction the Gullah people worked the land and became self sufficient and independent. They produced everything they needed and had all types of livestock's (cows, hogs, goats, oxen, chicken, etc.). They had smokehouses to cure their own meat and canned their own food. Some of the Gullah people became craftsmen and worked for Archer and Anna Huntington in producing the largest outdoor sculpture museum in America (Brookgreen Gardens). Brookgreen Gardens is a must see for any visitor to the Myrtle Beach grand strand area.

The early Gullah people had a strong and deep abiding faith, and the current church was built around 1880 (New Bethel Baptist Church). My father was born and raised in Annie Village on Sandy Island (village named after his mother). My uncle Samuel still resides in Annie Village. My father would often tell stories of life on the island and how he had to go to work at age thirteen to help his family after his father died. He worked many years on the island before migrating to Conway, a little town about thirty miles to the northwest. Although he had little formal education, he learned to read and write and was very learned and worked for the next fifty five years and retired at age sixty eight. The house he built in 1946 still stands today and is a legacy and beacon to his commitment to achievement.

Early Years –
In the early years the Gullah people worked the land on the rice plantations along what is called the waccamaw neck. The rice plantations were productive because of the skill of the workers and profitable because of the free slave labor. A number of wealthy rice planters had summer homes on the island for a number of years.

After emancipation changes came and many of the former slaves left the plantations for the mainland to find work. Many returned to work the fields and land for their own benefit, and after a few years some of them were able to purchase their own land. The rice planters could not pay the freed slaves what they could earn as laborers in the surrounding areas. The rice culture could not survive economically, and the rice plantation owners eventually sold their land to others (rich northerners).

A former slave foreman, Philip Washington, at the old Pipe Down plantation amassed enough money to purchase 382 acres from the widow of a plantation owner. The community of former slaves at Mt. Arena had worked the land for a number of years before becoming landowners. It is apparent that they were productive farmers and worked the land successfully and passed it down to their generations today. Philip Washington was an astute businessman, although he was

9

forbidden to read and write his legacy is very dominant on the island today. There are Freedman Bank records that show that he had an account and made deposits at the Freedman Bank in Charleston, S.C.

Just standing at the dock at Mt. Arena or strolling on the bank of the Waccamaw River you can feel the sense of history, and of your ancestors who strolled here centuries ago. There are many artifacts in and around Mt. Arena including old cemeteries. Their descendants still reside today on the same settlement where the Waccamaw River still flows not too far from their front doors. The river and the trees have seen many generations come and go.

It is a serene setting and sunset is particularly different from this perspective on the riverbank, perhaps each generation does see some things from a different perspective. During post-reconstruction the new landowners again made changes in the lives of the freed slaves. It was an agricultural society without slave labor and with a push toward more industry. The workers could make more as an industrial laborer than they could by working the land.

Archer and Anna Huntington bought Brookgreen Gardens along the waccamaw, and the blacks were trained as brick masons and built most of Brookgreen Gardens. Brookgreen Gardens now contains the largest outdoor collection of sculptures in America. Blacks also built Atalaya House at Huntington Beach State Park which is located right across the highway from Brookgreen Gardens. Post reconstruction brought about many changes, and smaller rice planting continued until the late forties and died out as a way of life with that generation.

Children still stroll and play along the banks of the Waccamaw River, and walk over to the old school yard and to the playground with a few basketball rims to play pick-up basketball. Some walk and stroll to the church and cemetery. Strolling on the island is wonderful in the fall and spring, as it gets kind of hot in the summertime.

Extended families are a tradition on the island, and the senior citizens have seen generations of their descendants live and play and roam on the island just as they did many decades ago. They are aware that they are living on a natural treasure with some of the most serene settings any eyes have been blessed to behold. No matter how many times you have seen the scenes or how long you have lived on the island, each sunset and new day brings new life and joy in the appreciation of nature's beauty and delight on the serene island. The Waccamaw River flows with a new message every day and the centuries old moss trees blow with the breeze on and from the river. It is hard to believe that you are only three miles away from the tourist's hotels, golf courses, shops and restaurants on highway 17.

People were Self Sufficient and Independent –
Families working the land were a tradition and way of life, and all families had their own vegetable gardens and various farm animals they needed such as, cows, oxen, goats, and hogs, chicken. They also caught and trapped deer, birds, wild turkeys, ducks, turtles and various wildlife. They also had all the fish they could catch including the popular shad. Fresh water fish is

wonderful and we had many a fresh water fish cookout, and that was really good eating. The river is wonderful and supplies food and abundant life. The shad fish comes to the fresh water at a certain time of the year to lay their eggs, as they are ocean fish.

The river can also be cruel, treacherous, and unpredictable and many residents have been drowned by various occurrences, such as large boats or ships passing by raising big waves, or logs or other obstacles in the river. The river flows where the river flows, and when you make it safely to the banks it's wonderful. The old timers would tell the youngsters that if you see an alligator (gator) resting on the banks of the river, just don't bother the gator and the gator won't bother you.

In the early days when the residents had only small row boats it was most dangerous. I remember my aunt coming down from Philadelphia to visit and she couldn't wait for the other residents to get off work and give her a ride across the river. I was with her to keep her company, and to my surprise she just figured out what boat belonged to her brother Samuel and we got in the boat and she rowed across the river all the way to Annie Village at the old boat dock.

That is an experience I will always remember, as she was also visiting my parents (her oldest brother) in Conway and wanted someone to keep her company on her journey to Sandy Island, and I was selected to accompany her. We just took a greyhound bus to Brookgreen Gardens and got off on US 17 and walked through Brookgreen Gardens to the Waccamaw River and the old landing.

It just took forever to row across and down the Waccamaw River from that old landing, and I really dreaded the boat ride. The river seemed even more treacherous then and the boats were so small it seemed like you were sitting on cardboard floating across the river. Every time those wooden oars hit the river I think my heart skipped many a beats. Sometimes I would just close my eyes for a few minutes hoping that when I opened them we would be close to shore. But more times than not I would only see the big river, and I could look in the distance and see some of the wetlands that were converted to rice fields in the 1800s' and the centuries old trees.

I never imagined that I would be able to see the same scenes today over five decades later. I was sure that development would come to the island and I would not see it in its same pristine setting decades later after I retired. I was delighted to see that the various attempts at development fail, as we have seen what development has done to other sea islands, as development brings condominiums, golf courses, and the local way of life destroyed forever.

Perhaps the biggest impact of development would have been on the senior citizens of the island. They have spent their entire life in isolation and remember and lived the early days over six decades ago when life was so different then, as they truly lived off the land. People were accustomed to living off the land and residing in small communities or towns. We now live in a 21st century technological society, and the elder residents can also maintain their old way of life on the island as they desire. I'm delighted that they got to keep their island in isolation and to continue on with their traditions.

With no bridge to the island the residents continue to make their way across the Waccamaw River and intercoastal waterway to get to and from the island. The only means of travel to and from the island for most residents is still by small boats, but now they have motors. The motorboats are a little larger than the old rowboats, but they are still small motorboats by today's standard.

I still don't like riding in the small motorboats and would prefer to ride in the school boat or the church boat that are larger. Now that most of the island is a preserve owned by the state this insures that there will be no development of the island. Some of the senior citizens said that in the past there was always talk throughout the years about putting a bridge on the island ever since they were kids. The senior citizens are now convinced that they will not see a bridge to the island, and most residents seem delighted that a bridge is not coming. In some households two and three generations reside, and the elders have passed on stories to their children and grandchildren on the traditions of Gullah life as passed down to them.

The main method of traveling on the island is still by walking, although there are a few old trucks and jeeps to drive on the few unpaved pathways and sandy roads. Residents frequently walk from the other two settlements to Mt. Arena and back. The residents of Annie Village and Georgia Hill have to dock their boats at the boat dock at Mt. Arena as there is no longer a boat dock near their settlements. A few have vehicles to drive to and from Mt. Arena, but others walk unless they are lucky enough to get a ride with someone who owns a vehicle and is heading in the same direction.

Everyone don't get off work at the same time, so they don't all arrive at the landing at the mainland or at the boat dock at Mt. Arena at the same time. Therefore it is often quicker to walk home to the other two settlements than to wait at Mt. Arena for someone to get off work and catch a ride with them. Most residents prefer it with no bridge, because a bridge would not guarantee a benefit to residents. Bridges to other islands have brought things to those islands that the natives didn't appreciate, want or need. They have been isolated for centuries and generations and are accustomed to living life as such, where the Waccamaw River flows by not too far from your front door and you can feel the cool summer breeze from the river. I truly enjoyed my summers on the island and hope for those days again.

The Sandy Island Landing

School Boat Docked at Sandy Islanding

The Sandy Island Landing is where the residents
of the island park their cars, as
there is no bridge to the island. They get
in their boats and go across the
Waccamaw River to get to the island.

A resident in his small motor boat leaving the
Sandy Island Landing, and going to go across
the Waccamaw River to his home on the island
after a trip to the mainland.

Crossing the Waccamaw River and approaching
the Mt. Arena boat dock on Sandy Island.
Residents dock their boats
here and go home to one of the Gullah
settlements on the island

My Summers on Sandy Island

I can remember my early days visiting on Sandy Island; I was amazed at the independence of the people on the island. Sometimes they didn't come to the mainland for months, as they had no need to leave the island. I can remember playing in and around Annie Village, and walking over to Red Sand Hill taking in the sights of the moss trees. Cows were nearby with bells around their necks. We could walk all the way down by the water's edge to one of the landing that the residents of Annie Village and Georgia Hill used. Georgia Hill was another residential area just above Annie Village.

I can remember my grandmother planting rice and working the rice fields and harvesting the rice. (My grandfather died in 1923). I remember my grandmother shucking the rice in wooden objects, etc. My grandmother also had large crops of peanuts; the green peanuts were piled in stacks to dry. They produced more than they could consume, so some was shipped to market in Georgetown, about fifteen miles away on the mainland. Some sacks of peanuts were also sent to my father in Conway as the extended family concept was still in effect.

I had some wonderful summers on Sandy Island with the Gullah people. We are all Gullah people, but the people on the sea islands are referred to as salt water Gullah, and the Gullah people on the mainland (such as me) are referred to as fresh water Gullah. We would sometimes walk to Mount Arena to visit other people on the island. Mount Arena is about two miles from Annie Village, and Mount Arena is the largest Gullah residential area on the island. The early school was located in Mount Arena, but as you got older you had to take the school boat to the mainland to go to school. My cousins still reside in Mount Arena right by the side of the Waccamaw River. They can still watch the sun set on the banks of the raging river just as have been done by each preceding generation for years.

I was especially saddened when my grandmother passed away. I can remember it just like it was yesterday. I was very young but I can remember the casket on the oxen cart and two oxen's pulling the cart from Annie Village to Blain (another settlement on Sandy Island). Everyone had to walk behind the oxen cart all the way to the church because there were no motor vehicles on the island in the early fifties. My grandmother is buried in Blain cemetery on Sandy Island.

I can remember the funeral at the church very vividly, although it was 1951. There were some tremendous speakers in that church, and I remember one speaker in particular, I don't recall his name, just the wisdom he imparted. He went on to remind us that God did not give us a mother to remain with us here on earth forever, but just for a while to guide us and help us along in this wayfaring world. That God knows when to call our parents home for their rest, and will keep us and guide us through life's journey ahead, if we just trust and believe in him.

It was evident to me as a young child that these people had something that was truly divine. I didn't understand at the time how a people could have such a strong faith in the midst of such isolation. Their wisdom, knowledge and understanding shone through as it has for generations. The elder generation has all but died out now but their legacy lives on in their descendants.

I enjoyed some wonderful summers on Sandy Island with the Gullah people. The early school was located in the Mt. Arena section of the island and the teachers lived in the community and were very dedicated and committed to seeing that the children got a very good education to prepare them for life's challenges ahead. Therefore I am certain that the Gullah people of today will make it through the long day just as their ancestors did. Even though they didn't have many luxuries in those early days, they had a deep and abiding fortitude that kept them focused on the straight and narrow. I know there's a new dawn, and I will continue in the spirit of the Gullah people.

My father was born and raised in Annie Village on Sandy Island; he migrated to Conway, a small town about thirty miles northwest of the island to work and live and raises his family. His wife was from Plantersville, just across the Great Pee Dee River on the west side of Sandy Island, and she had migrated to Conway to work. Her best friend was my father's sister, and they met when my mother came to Sandy Island with her best friend while my father was still living on Sandy Island. My father's sister had migrated to Myrtle Beach to work but went back to Sandy Island often. So my mother and her best friend eventually became sister in laws.

Conway is a small Riverfront historic old town established or settled around 1735 as a borough. The Waccamaw River runs all the way to Conway with the intercoastal waterway close by. Conway is still growing and is a little larger now but still has a small town atmosphere and not at all like the Myrtle Beach grand strand area where tourism is the main industry. Conway was fairly rural four decades ago and tobacco and cotton were main crops that the farmers depended on for a living. Many of the residents in town would work the summers in the tobacco and cotton fields to get money for the school semester.

A number of other Gullah people and families had also migrated from the Sea Islands and came inland a bit to work and live. You could always tell them from the locals because they had a different accent, and they always remembered their roots. They spoke with an African dialect referred to as Gullah-Geechee, and some people referred to them as Geechees, but they didn't seem to mind as they just kept focused.

You could also tell them by their excellence in school, as most of them seemed to achieve quite well and naturally. They were also very creative in the arts and the bands, especially playing the drums. They were very good athletes and many were outstanding football players who excelled and went on to Play College and professionally.

I enjoyed going to school in Conway in a community with a large number of Gullah people who had migrated to the area. The community was called the Whittemore Community and it had the only high school that we could attend in the fifties. The teachers and students were extremely dedicated and motivated. Most of the students went on to become outstanding citizens and leaders in all professions and led productive lives. I always looked forward to the end of the school year because that meant it was summer and my parents would let me spend most of the summer on Sandy Island. We were too young to work and with us kids staying on the island in the summer meant that both of our parents could work at the same time. During the other months of the year our parents did not work the same shift when we were young.

I would usually arrive on Sandy Island on a warm sunny afternoon, most likely a Saturday. We took a greyhound bus ride from Conway to the entrance of Brookgreen Gardens on US 17, and then a long walk through Brookgreen Gardens, to the old boat landing at the Waccamaw River. Then we got into the small row boat and sit forever while my uncle rowed the boat across and down the river to the other old boat landing a good little piece east of Annie Village. Then we had to walk to Annie Village lugging all our belongings and bags of groceries.

It was a little tiring but we endured because we knew we had a lot to look forward to in the days ahead. There were no cars, electricity or running water on the island in the early fifties as the island was totally unchanged and really isolated in those days. As we walked to Annie Village we would see the cows, oxen, goats and live stocks roaming freely and grazing, which kept the grass from overgrowing.

My grandmother had a big spread of land in Annie Village (named after her) and her sister owned another big spread adjacent to her. My grandmother and her sister were both widows with large extended families. Some of their sons lived in the Village with their families.

Large families were a custom in those days, and there were plenty of us kids to roam and play and explore the area. Just outside of Annie Village were a lot of woods, even unto this day, and we would roam and play in the woods. We couldn't get lost because the Waccamaw River flowed on the east side of the woods and the few pathways and sandy roads were not too far from the river. Everything was near the river including small rice fields at the inlets, and the cows seem to linger not too far from the river.

When we strayed too far into the woods we could always listen for the bells that the cows wore around their necks and just head for the bells and that would lead us in the direction of home. When we heard the bells we knew we were getting closer to Red Sand Hill the place we often played at. It was between Annie Village and the old boat dock, and we always found our way back home.

We played a lot, but we also had little chores, like getting firewood from the surrounding woods that contained an endless supply of firewood. We had no heating bills in those days. As we gathered firewood we would sometimes see tracks of large turtles (called cooters) and we would follow the tracks until we caught the big turtles. There were some really big turtles on the island; some were a foot or more in length. We would bring home some extra firewood because we were going to have some cooter stew tonight.

We would also track small games, such as, rabbits, squirrels, birds, and fished in shallow water for the small fishes. Annie Village and its surroundings were a nice place to live and play, and we didn't even seem to notice that we didn't have some of the luxuries that were taken for granted by those who lived on the mainland. I didn't miss not having electric lights or running water, although in my early years in Conway we didn't have electric lights or running water. We had kerosene lamps and two old time pumps in our back yard. On Sandy Island they had lamps and deep water wells, and that deep water well water was so cool and refreshing.

This was before the days of high pollution when the air was pure and clean and healthy. Annie Village and its surroundings were my joy and delight, and the old moss trees in and around Red Sand Hill seemed so pristine, even though they were centuries old they were still in their natural setting and environment that they had been in for centuries. It wasn't until it was many years later that I began to fully realize and appreciate what I had the honor and privilege to experience.

Annie Village has always been my favorite location, even unto this day, I will always cherish my experiences there and will always remember them and am grateful that I passed that way with so many wonderful people. We would sometimes walk up to the next little settlement just above Annie Village. That settlement was called Georgia Hill, named after its founder, and she had a little store on the premises where we could go and buy a candy bar for a nickel or a dime.

When we got tired of roaming and playing in the surrounding areas of our village we would walk to Mt. Arena the largest and main settlement on the island. More families and children were at Mt. Arena, and therefore we had more people to play with. The old school and playground were also located at Mt. Arena.

We could also explore the surrounding woods along the pathways as we walked, and many a time we would find turtle tracks or other games and wild life to try and catch.

It was a lot of fun walking the island in those days, especially along the shores and bank of the Waccamaw River. The river and inlets, marshes and shallow waters were a lot cleaner and clear in those days and supported more abundant marine life. I was very young then but I still remember those days and the difference is striking when compared with today. And now that development is not coming to the island I am sure that it won't be too long before the island returns to a more wonderful condition as I spend more time there.

The Old Sandy Island School –
The old school still stands in its original location after all these years since we walked and played in its schoolyard. It now looks more historic than ever, and a lot of history is in that old building and if it could talk I would listen forever. Meetings are held in the old school now and then and when restored it would make a wonderful community center and cultural center for residents of the island.

One of the teachers who taught in that old school is a cousin of mine, and many of the former students came back to the Sandy Island Family reunion and gave testimony as to how the teachers there had prepared them well for the world outside. They recalled how the training they received had prepared them to be successful in life all over the country and world. One of the former students is now a judge in Georgetown, about fifteen miles south of the island. The old Sandy Island school prepared the students well before they went on to high school at Howard High in Georgetown or Whittemore High in Conway.

When the children were ready to leave the old Sandy Island School and go to high school they had to take the school boat from the Mt. Arena boat dock and travel across the Waccamaw River to the Sandy Island Landing and then take a school bus to the mainland school. Now that the old school is closed all the children on the island must go to mainland schools, and they seem to enjoy riding on the Prince Washington, the state's only school boat. Rain or shine and in all types of weather the children take the school boat to the mainland to go to school.

The current generation is being educated on the mainland with a more diverse student body and access to more technology, especially computers. This was quite a difference from the education of their ancestors who were taught in the old school, or in the homes of teachers who lived on the island. Some of these children are the sixth and seventh generation of the settlers who first settled Mt. Arena.

One of the Old School boat's Skelton can be seen at low tide at Mt. Arena, its wooden hull is almost gone, but you can see traces of it at low tide. The prior school boats only exist in pictures, now that they are buried beneath the Waccamaw River, and a part of history lost forever. The island has remained undeveloped for centuries and many things are the same on the island. But each generation is different, and as the prior generations rarely left the island because they were self sufficient and independent. They could live off the land and could grow most of what they needed, as farming and fishing gave them a good life. Their ties to the island ran deep even though many of them had to work from sun up to sun down, they loved the island.

The young generation now works on the mainland and commutes back and forth to the island every workday. The young generation must now compete and work in a 21st century technological society, even though they choose to continue to live on the island that hasn't changed much in centuries. The ties of the young generation to the island and its traditions are also very strong, and they do not want the island to change by development, even though their lives have changed. Their Gullah roots are on the island and will always be a part of them.

The old Sandy Island School would make a wonderful Gullah Cultural and Heritage Center – Community Center on Sandy Island, and compliment what the church is doing on the island. The church was established about 1880 and is located a little outside of Mt. Arena. These facilities would just begin to tell the history and stories of the people who fought so hard to maintain their way of life through many adverse conditions. This would be a testimony as to what hard work and perseverance can accomplish for a people working together for the good of all. The church on the island has been the one stable institution for the people and has kept the culture intact as well as given spiritual uplifting and direction to generations of the Gullah people. Their faith has always remained strong.

A Deep and Abiding Faith

The church was established by the ancestors of the people that attend that church today. Much was accomplished by men and women who didn't have a lot to begin with. They didn't have a lot of formal education to begin with. They had limited access to educational and economic opportunities, and limited access to information. But as one of the senior citizens told a youngster, you have education given by man, but I have wisdom and understanding given by God; I realized immediately that Proverbs 2:6 and 4:7 says the exact same thing. And then the senior citizen told the young person that you will never know what I know. We were at a cookout at Mt. Arena just sitting on the porch talking and exchanging stories near the bank of the river.

Some of the seniors on the island have lived in the same location or area for over eight decades, and have seen much come and go, and many are still very keen. They have some unique insights and their faith is very strong, and you can just feel the tremendous tranquility, peace and security they impart. They have seen many sunrises and sunsets looking out across the river, and they will impart knowledge and wisdom to those willing to listen.

I enjoy and look forward to visiting the island for the various cookouts and reunions, just to see, talk and listen to the senior citizens, especially my uncle; for they are a wealth of information and are eager to share it with those who are willing to listen. It's a joy and wonderful experience just to sit at the picnic table under the big tree at Mt. Arena and listen to the senior citizens talk about the history of the island as they themselves have experienced it.

Some of the seniors didn't remember my name at first, but they could look at me and they knew that I was a son of my father. They all knew my father very well and just knew I was in the same mold and I have been told that I look like a Pyatt. They had a lot of information and made sure I got all I asked for.

Some of the senior citizens have been going to the same church on the island for over eight decades. It's a country church surrounded by a lot of woods, but the people go to church dressed in their Sunday best, just like folks in larger cities. You would think that being so isolated that they would go to church dressed more casual to better manipulate the rough terrain and sandy roads and pathways. But that's not the case and many walk those sandy roads and pathways all the way to the church. The church is located outside Mt. Arena about a third of the way to Annie Village. There are many a lumps and bumps in those roads and pathways, even unto this day, as they are still unimproved.

I can remember walking to church from Annie Village over fifty years ago on these same sandy roads and pathways. Back then there were no cars or trucks on the island and the oxen carts were our transportation when it was needed. Nowadays some people get to church by driving one of the few trucks or jeeps available, or you may be lucky enough to catch a ride. But the people have always made it to that church dressed in what we call their "Sunday go to meeting clothes" stepping proudly.

At least there are a few vehicles on the island for some of the people to use today in their daily lives. But fifty years ago when I spent my summers on the island the oxen carts were the main and only means of travel. The oxen carts were not used on a regular basis because the sandy roads meant that the oxen could not walk very fast in the sandy sand, and walking would get you to your destination quicker. Whenever we did take the oxen cart there were too many of us to ride all at once, and we would have to take turns walking and riding.

The oxen cart was used primarily as a hearse for funerals back in those days, it seemed odd but it worked quite well. The people were very good in using what they had to get the job or task done, and they usually got it done quite well. Whatever needed to be done seemed to always get done.

Time has passed as many years have passed, and some things have changed, but some things remain the same on the isolated island. Time has brought tremendous technological changes in our lives no matter where we live or how isolated we are, with the computer and television we can get news instantly from all over the world. Some people go all over the world getting educated but never able to come to the knowledge of the truth. A study and knowledge of ones' culture and heritage may teach you how the elder generations acquired so much knowledge, wisdom and understanding in what appeared to be an impossible situation to outsiders.

I could see the fortitude of faith in the Gullah people in isolation, and especially in my parents and in their character; and I knew early on that they got what they had from a higher source. I was very young then, but I realized that they did not have the educational or economic opportunities that I had and would get. I thought they had limited access to information, but they had a type of community grapevine that kept them well informed on certain critical matters. It was later that I realized that they had the experience of life with wisdom, knowledge and understanding, a main reason I always sought their advice for over five decades.

The Gullah peoples' spirituality always came through strongly in their daily lives and character. They had what it took to survive and excel in their generation without falling for many of the snares of the world. That was a major trait in many of them and they could separate the facts from the folly when any type of con man came around peddling some type of nonsense.

I knew it was their deep faith and belief in God and work, for they did not rely on handouts and prided themselves in being self sufficient and independent. They believed in working and supporting themselves and their families, a far cry from what a lot of youngsters are doing today. That was one of the main traits that I noticed at a young age, and I wanted to be self sufficient and independent too. They adhered to what was written centuries ago; "That the man that tilleth his land shall have plenty of bread, but he that followeth after vain persons shall have poverty enough", Proverbs 28:19. These people believed and lived their faith and were not afraid to work hard for a living and accepted no handouts. Whatever they got they most certainly earned it and more. This was the value system that was passed down to them, and I'm glad they passed it down to me. It was said a long time ago that a workman should be worthy of his meat, that's what the disciples were told before they went out into the world on their mission.

That is the value system that I took out into the world with me from the Gullah people. I can truly say that I've never accepted one dime of government handouts, and worked over forty two years and retired to a good life in the spirit of the Gullah people. I have never regretted working hard for everything I got and enjoyed working for my keeps. I learned at a very young age on Sandy Island what hard work and perseverance can do to enable you to become self sufficient and independent.

The institution of marriage was also sacred and cherished by the Gullah people on Sandy Island, and divorce was almost unheard of with the elder generations. When they said till death do us part, that's exactly what they meant, and that's exactly what they did. They believed that "what God hath joined together, let no man put asunder". And they practiced and lived their belief and treated everyone as family.

There were many large extended families on the island, and it seemed like everyone knew each other and that we all were family and everyone enjoyed helping each other. When we were roaming and playing along the way and got tired and wanted to take a break, we could just go sit on anyone's front porch and rest a while. We would come in out the rain on anyone's porch or just sit and drink some water.

I did not know everyone's first names since I was only on the island mostly on my summer break from school. But they always treated me as one of them, and the same hospitality and concern for others is apparent today each time I visit the island. As I go to the island to visit, my cousin now takes me across the river in his motorboat;

the residents will come up to me and know that I'm a Pyatt. They even lend a hand in helping me out of the boat onto the landing to ensure that I don't slip and fall into the river.

They just have an inherent genuine concern for helping people, especially visitors to the island. Although I'm now more than just a visitor because they know I come to the island more often now, especially to attend the various cookouts and reunions. I enjoy the various events they have at Mt. Arena where everyone comes and there is an exchange of stories, or just to listen to the stories by others. The residents are familiar and know their island, and when they say don't go in that direction I most certainly follow their advice.

This is where I started from and it's a delight to return to Sandy Island as much as possible. I know that it was the faith and belief of these people that gave me added inspiration, with my faith and belief and trust in God that have brought me through the years and back to this wonderful point in time. We know we have more work to do, especially in helping the young generation get through some of the hurdles they still face today. We will accept our responsibilities and obligations in these days ahead just as we have always done in the days and years gone by. We know and are living proof of what can be accomplished when we continue in the Gullah tradition of achievement.

The history of the Gullah people is truly remarkable and should be remembered forever. We shall continue to pass it down from generation to generation just as it was passed down to us. It's a continuing and lasting blessing.

They seemed to have all the secrets for success, even on that isolated island, they may have been isolated but their philosophy was right on and timely. My parents understood that they should study and work; that it was not sufficient to just pray and hope for the best, and that you had to actually study the Big Book in order to pass that final test. They always studied the scriptures and kept abreast of current events in the world, and passed such habits on to us.

My father even had a complete set of encyclopedias in the fifties that he studied before I got to high school, and I'm sure he read every one of them. I had additional resources before I got to high school, as many a day I would find myself on the back porch going through and reading those books. I knew that the principles they lived by were from a higher source and I wanted to tap into their source.

They knew that they had to study and work to receive benefits and rewards; they knew that just being saved was not enough, and that they should move on to perfection. These are the exact principles documented in II Timothy 2:15 and James 2:17-26; they understood and lived by the "Word of Truth". This was and still is a major trademark or tradition of the Gullah people, to live in obedience to God's Principles. Many of the families have attended the same church for generations.

Those Principles have carried them through some difficult times that I have witnessed and was amazed at their fortitude. It was readily apparent that their spiritual belief rested on a very solid foundation. They did not just give lip service to the Commandments and Principles, they obeyed and lived them. The community was truly a "Bible Belt Community". They made sure that their children went to Sunday school and church every Sunday, and I enjoyed going to Sunday school and church every Sunday in the Gullah community. I particularly enjoyed the Bible School we had at the beginning of the summer before I went to spend the rest of the summer on Sandy Island.

There were Jubilee singers in the churches in those days, partly because there was a lack of musical instruments due to a lack of funds. But Jubilee singers didn't need music, as they would make their own music by clapping their hands and patting their feet to create the perfect rhythm to accompany them. I only wish that I had a video camcorder back in those days to have recorded such inspirational music of that era. I especially liked the Sundays when I knew that the Jubilee singers would be the main choir that month.

Sundays were sacred in the "Bible Belt Community" and after church we were supposed to rest and not work or play ball. As a youngster growing up in the Whittemore community we liked to play baseball every day during the spring and summer, but I was not allowed to play ball on Sunday. On Sunday afternoons my parents would often sit on the front porch to relax, and I couldn't figure out how to get my baseball glove past them so that I could go play ball. I finally decided to place my baseball glove on my bicycle seat and sit on it and just ride out of the front yard.

My ingenuity would have worked just fine, but there was a fence around the house and yard. As I approached the front gate on my bicycle I was covering my baseball glove by sitting on it, but I couldn't reach the latch on the gate sitting down, so I had to rise up just for a moment on my bicycle. And as soon as I rose up guess what fell to the ground, yes my baseball glove, and I never tried to pull that trick again.

There really is "Only One Way"' the right way, and even nature itself teaches us right from wrong. The discipline and direction I received at a young age kept me in the right direction and prepared me well to become a success in life and a productive citizen. I have seen many people who have gone in other directions and become stuck in a mud-pile, trapped in a quagmire and untold folly. I learned a long time ago to apply scriptural solutions to whatever problems you may have, and I have always found it to be a panacea.

It has kept me from many snares along the way. I always received good and pragmatic advice even at a young age. My parents were very good at explaining to me the difference between good tradition and bad tradition that should be avoided. They were also very good at analyzing the local political establishment and telling us how certain laws would be enforced. They knew what local leaders would do and which ones could be trusted and which one's to be avoided. Even in retirement my mother would go to the courthouse and sit in and observe various trials. Her very keen insight was very unique, and I know we will meet again, for my generation is the fig tree generation.

As the preacher states, "one generation passeth away, and another generation cometh: but the earth abideth forever", Ecclesiastes 1:4. "All the rivers run into the sea; yet the sea is not full; unto the place from whence the rivers come, thither they return again", Ecclesiastes

1:7. In the sweat of thy face shall thou eat bread, till thou return to the ground; for out of it wast thou taken: for dust thou art, and unto dust shalt thou return", Genesis 3:19. "Then shall the dust return to the earth as it was: and the spirit shall return unto God who gave it", Ecclesiastes 12:7.

The Gullah people deeply believed in God's Principles, and so do I, for they are the "Word of Truth" and have guided me through some difficult times, and kept me from the midst of chaos and confusion. They knew that God's love was a true love, and not a perverted love; they "loved in truth and in deed, and did not love in word and in tongue", I John 3:18. It was apparent then so many years ago on that isolated island; that they had found and knew the truth, and the truth made them free. They Practiced Truth, Taught Truth, and Knew the Truth.

That generation has mostly passed on now, and I am thankful that I can also get the truth from the same Higher Source that gave it to them. I know it works because I have seen what it did for them.

It is a surety and a truth as stated in the Proverbs 28:19, that "he that tilleth his land shall have plenty of bread: but he that followeth after vain persons shall have poverty enough. Therefore I will seek wisdom, knowledge and understanding from that same Higher Source. Those of the elder generation were not strategically misadjusted, they didn't have degrees, but they had economic skills and knew how to work the land. There were some former slaves within a decade or so after being freed were master farmers and produced much on land their purchased from their former owners.

They settled and developed their own communities for themselves, a far cry from the mindset of today in many communities. They did not continue to beg and seek government aid and wait for others to do for them what they should do for themselves. They had an economic agenda for the economic development of their community, and pooled resources when necessary for the betterment of the community.

They used logic and common sense, for they knew that you will eventually have to suffer the natural and probable consequences of your actions. It carried them through some dark days, and when they reached critical crossroads, they knew what direction to take. They knew right from wrong and how to discern the righteous from the wicked, and didn't mistake folly for wisdom. They did not judge others, but they knew how to judge a tree by the fruit it bears.

They had goals and objectives and knew what to do to improve their condition in life, and knew the secrets for success. They had the proper **Attitude, Conduct** and **Environment (ACE)**.

Attitude - Their Attitude was conducive to Accomplishments.
Conduct - Their Conduct was not detrimental to Progress.
Environment - Their Environment even in isolation was ideal and protected them from outside Negative Influences.

A Small Boat Coming to Mt. Arena
Bringing Residents Home

THE SANDY ISLAND SCHOOL BOAT

The Prince Washington (The Sandy Island
School Boat) Is the only school boat in the state
of South Carolina

THE OLD SANDY ISLAND SCHOOL

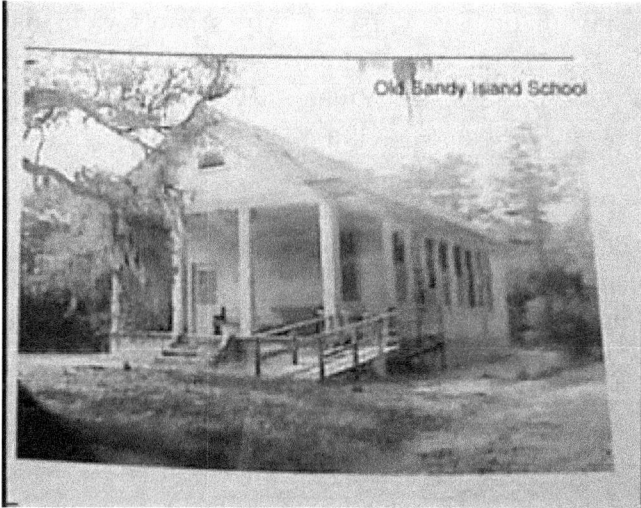

The Old Sandy Island School still stands today in its original location. A truly historic old building.

Other Stories

As a Freshwater Gullah I grew up on one of the mainland towns called Conway located about thirty miles northwest of Sandy Island. I didn't have a lot of the hardships that the Saltwater Gullah children had growing up on Sandy Island. My schools were only about a ten minute walk from our house. My cousins who grew up in Annie Village had to walk about two miles to get to their school in Mt. Arena.

One of my cousins and me are about six months apart, and he would tell me stories about how they had to get up early in the morning, rain or shine, to get ready for the long sandy walk to school in Mt. Arena. And when they were old enough to go to school on the mainland they had to walk all the way from Annie Village to the Mt. Arena boat dock to catch the school boat. The Mt. Arena boat dock was a bit farther away from the Sandy Island School. The school boat took them across the Waccamaw River to the Sandy Island Landing where they had to take a school bus to get to school further on the mainland. The school bus would take them to the old Howard High School in Georgetown about fifteen miles away. A long, long day.

I was amazed at how those Gullah children on Sandy Island could endure the hardships and obstacles in getting a high school education and still not fall behind. They were very fortunate to have had some extremely dedicated teachers who were willing to go that extra mile when needed. My cousin transferred to Whittemore High School in Conway with me after he moved to Myrtle Beach. There was a high school in Myrtle Beach in those days but the Gullah children could not attend the only high school in Myrtle Beach. My cousin and I both graduated together over four decades ago with good grades. We both went on to have successful careers, and are now happily retired and enjoying life even more knowing how far we have come from.

It is amazing what hard work and a desire to succeed and be successful can do for a person in the midst of apparent difficulties and obstacles. We always found a way to get what we wanted, and set goals that we wanted to achieve, and did achieve. Our parents and teachers prepared us well and gave us a very strong foundation to meet the challenges that were to come. That is a Gullah tradition that is alive and well on the island, and is instilled in the children on the island by the adults.

There are many stories that I remember from my days and summers on Sandy Island, such as:

> Days at Annie Village
> Outside Annie Village
> Hanging Out at Red Sand Hill
>   (Fishing, Hunting, Smokehouses)
> The Old Boat Dock
> The Big Dinners at Annie Village
> Playing at Mt. Arena

Almost everyone had a story to tell at some point in time somewhere, at home or some event or cookout, or just sitting on the banks of the river passing the time away. It was a tremendous experience and provided memories that will last a lifetime.

Days at Annie Village

But all the days were not filled with the struggle just to get to school on the mainland. At least the children didn't have to work hard full time jobs as their parents did for the wealthy plantation owners. The children and my cousins at Annie Village would have to get firewood from the surrounding areas, and help out most at harvest time. They helped stack and shuck peanuts when they were taken from the ground. They also shucked and beat rice in those old big wooden look like bowls, as I referred to such wooden bowls.

The rice grew as a grain stalk and was harvested as a stalk, and the rice had to be separated from the stalk. The children would help care for and feed the live stocks; cows were on open graze, but the children helped milk the cows and goats, fed the hogs, helped with the garden for food and did whatever else was necessary as directed by the adults. The children did have responsibilities for the work assigned to them, and even though it was not considered full time work we enjoyed working to help out.

It was good healthy work and very rewarding to work the land and live off the land in our own village. The adults knew when to plant, what to plant and how to prepare the land to produce at its optimum. They made home made fruit cakes using the pecans and walnuts from the pecan trees and walnut trees in the yard. They made their own butter and ice cream and soap; and made and canned and jarred many other goodies to live on during the off season and winter. We also made our own refreshments from the many grapevines and blackberries all around.

They produced everything they needed to survive, and I do not recall ever lacking anything the many summers I spent on the island as I was growing up. I did not miss not being on the mainland at home in Conway, or any other so called luxury at that time, like electric lights. The clear night sky and stars provided adequate light for me.

The adults, especially my grandmother knew what herbs or leaves to collect and put them together to beat the juice out of them to use as medicine for various injuries and ailments. I never got sick on the island and at the change of seasons we were always given the proper homemade medicines. Sometimes in the summer the children would love to go and play bare feet, and some of them unintentionally would step in stagnant rainwater and get what was called ground itch. My grandmother knew how to use a paddle to beat their feet before putting the proper herbal leaves beaten on their feet wrapping it appropriately.

It appeared to me that the secret was not only in knowing what herbs or leaves to combine, but also how to beat them properly in order to get the juice from the herbal or leaves. My cousin stepped on a rusty nail one day as we were playing, and it was a fairly deep injury. My grandmother placed the proper herbal leaves and their juices on the injury and bandaged his foot, and he was well and up and running around in a few days. It was rare that they had to take someone to a doctor.

Days at Annie Village were wonderful and we played mostly on my grandmother's portion of the village. My grandmother's sister and some of her descendants resided on the other portion of the village. Annie Village was settled by two brothers who had married two sisters (my grandmother and her sister). The two brothers were deceased before I was born, my grandfather died in 1923 when my father was only 13 years old. The eldest generation I knew at Annie Village was my grandmother and my grandmother's sister.

In the early fifties when I spent my summers on the island my grandmother's three daughters and oldest son had already migrated away to live and work. My uncle and aunt had a house next to my grandmother's house, and there were many grandchildren there. My grandmother's sister had two sons, but only one of her sons and his wife resided in Annie Village. We also played outside the village.

Georgia Hill, Outside Annie Village

Playing in Annie Village was wonderful and we would often venture outside of the village to play in the surrounding areas. If we wanted to play with other kids nearby we would walk up to Georgia Hill where other children lived with their parents. Georgia Hill was located on a slight incline above Annie Village, but not really on a hill. Walking up any sandy slight incline sometimes feels like a big hill. If we had an extra nickel or a dime we would go the little store there on this side of the island.

The store was a little hut owned by Georgia and she would open up only when someone came by to buy something. It was not a store that was intended to make a profit, but only for the convenience of the local residents. If someone wanted something extra or ran out of something, they could get it at the store on Georgia Hill.

We went to Georgia Hill mostly to hang out and socialize and play with the other kids. All the children were well mannered and treated you just like you were their brother or sister. The main thing I remember is that they were always helpful, and it rarely occurred to me that there were no police on the island. Disputes were rare as there were rules that were established by our elders and we knew what the rules were, even though they were not written down.

We knew what we were supposed to do and what we should not do and we knew the consequences of not obeying the elders or any adult giving us proper direction. We didn't have any uniformed police on the island, but we had discipline and a sense of direction, as the elders and adults led by example. Even back in Conway I was more afraid of being disciplined by the adults than I was afraid of the police. I knew that the major concern of the adults were our well being. We also would hang out at Red Sand Hill, another area outside Annie Village.

Hanging Out at Red Sand Hill

When the children of Annie Village wanted to just hang out and play by themselves they would often go to Red Sand Hill, a serene setting a few hundred yards just east of Annie Village. Red Sand Hill was known for its unusually sandy sand and old moss trees, and the inlet and marsh was on one of its borders. It was a natural and pristine setting with clearing enough from the surrounding woods and wetlands.

The cows would be grazing or wading in the marshes not too far from shore. The cows grazing kept the area from overgrowing back in those days; it is a little overgrown now that the cows are not permitted to roam freely. Ants and their mounds would be on the ground with fire ants that were red, and if you stuck your feet or hand in their ant mound they would bite you so that you felt it. That is why it is called Red Sand Hill, for the red fire ants, not because the sand is red.

The clearing was enough for us to play catch with a ball and not get too close to the cows grazing because a bull was among the cows. I kept a close watch because I couldn't tell which one was the bull from a distance, but my cousins knew how to tell which one was the bull from a distance. I just know that I was told not to wear red clothing when we went to play at Red Sand Hill because the bull might be there grazing, and the bull didn't like red clothing.

One day we were playing at Red Sand Hill and one of the girls from the mainland had a red bow or ribbon in her hair. She apparently had forgotten that it was in her hair, but the bull noticed it from afar and started a slow charge. We ran away of course but couldn't figure out why the bull was charging as we knew not to wear red clothing. After a few charges by the bull, my cousin noticed that the girl had a red ribbon in her hair toward the back of her head. We didn't see the red ribbon at first, but the bull surely did, and came a charging at us all.

We respected the bull even more and never did anything again to upset the bull or invade its territory. We all just existed together at Red Sand Hill, everyone had their territory carved out, and the cows and bull had their piece of territory on their side of the hill. Even the red ants had their own little domain in their mounds and they didn't bite you until you encroached upon their territory. With the bull and cows on their space or territory, and the goats and hogs on their area, we could go to one edge of Red Sand Hill at the inlet where the water was shallow enough for us to fish for some of the small fishes there.

The water was clear and shallow as it reached the sandy shore. We could see the smaller fishes as they swam in the shallow waters and could wade in among them, as they didn't seem to mind. The fishes looked so fresh and edible, and we would try to reach down and catch them, and then you would find out how fast they were. We would sharpen hard sticks and use it to fish in the shallow water, and if you were patient and quick you could spear some small fishes over the course of the afternoon. We caught our fair share and had many a nice fresh water fish fries as we picnicked on our side of the island. That is really good healthy eating and the supply of fishes seemed endless as long as you were willing to fish you could catch yourself a meal.

On other days we would just go swimming in the shallow waters right beside the small fishes called minnows. It was a good place to learn how to swim because the water was too shallow to drown us. I took many a swimming lessons at the inlet from my older cousins. Red Sand Hill was the place to be on our portion of the island to enjoy a good outing in a natural environment. Now there are other historic areas not too far from Red Sand Hill, such as the old boat dock that was once the main landing dock for people on our part of the island, it is only memories now.

The Old Boat Dock

The inlet led back to the Waccamaw River and the old boat dock that was just east of Red Sand Hill. We would take the pathways from Red Sand Hill to the old boat dock to frolic around and fish and pass time. The old boat dock was where the residents of Annie Village and Georgia Hill docked their boats in the fifties when I spent my summers on the island. There was no Sandy Island Landing back in those days, as everyone had to go through Brookgreen Gardens to cross over to the island.

In those days the residents only had small rowboats, and I can remember sitting in those small boats for what seemed like forever as my uncle rowed us across the Waccamaw River. Once we got to the Sandy Island side of the river we would row closer to the shore just in case a larger boat was coming down the river. I remember the wooden paddles that were used to row the boat and how the rower leaned way back as he completed his row. It took some physical manpower to row that much almost every day. But they had no choice because they were so isolated. It was a longer trip for the residents of Annie Village and Georgia Hill because they were about two miles upriver from Mt. Arena.

I remember many days arriving at the old boat dock after getting off the greyhound bus on US 17, and walking through Brookgreen Gardens to the dock there, and then coming across the Waccamaw River to the old boat dock near Red Sand Hill. After my uncle would carefully maneuver and dock the boat we would carefully make our way onto the dock and away from the river as quickly as possible.

We then had to walk about a quarter of a mile to get to Annie Village. There were a lot of old moss trees all along the way, and it looked like the moss trees had many stories to tell after being there all those years, watching so many generations come and go on those same beaten pathways and sandy roads.

I would often look at those old moss trees and wonder just how many souls they have seen trek these pathways over the centuries. Their serenity was very calm and peaceful, even unto this day, and at times you can feel a special aura in that area. The old wooden boat dock has all but rotten away now and the overgrowth has all but covered up a deep part of that history on this side of the island, but stories are still passed down to the younger generations.

Over the years we have always gone back to the old boat dock, to where it once stood just to pause and reflect on times past. We had some good days at that old dock, no matter how isolated it was, it was a part of us as we grew up and played near that part of the river. After playing all over the area we always looked forward to going back to Annie Village for lunch and dinner because the food was so well prepared. We had all types of fresh meat and vegetables that were locally grown. I remember a favorite of mine was special sweet molasses bread made with the honey from local bee hives.

There were many a days that produce grown on this side of the island was shipped to market on the mainland from that old boat dock. Peanuts were a big and good crop in the early fifties, and sacks of peanuts were shipped to market in Georgetown. As we went to and from the old boat dock from Annie Village we would pass near the old smoke house. The smoke house was always filled with meat a-curing, and was not too far from the big house.

I remember my uncle and others slaughtering cows and hogs near the inlet where there was plenty of water to clean the meat and prepare it for curing. I remember seeing long sides of meat hanging in the smokehouse a-curing. You could smell the meat a-curing as soon as you opened the smoke house door, and we knew that it would not be too long before we would be having some of this fresh meat for dinner at the big house.

Dinners at Annie Village

We would periodically go to the smokehouse to get some meat for cooking at the big house for dinner. This was a chore that we really enjoyed and we made sure we had gotten extra firewood, and we had some extra firewood stacked away to keep it dry just in case it decided to rain for a few days. We made sure that we had everything we needed in advance because we didn't want anything to interfere with our evening meal, and it was a treat we always looked forward to every day.

Dinner was always a big occasion every day with three generations gathering around the house and porch ready to eat. There were so many of us kids visiting in the summers that we couldn't all sit at the same table for dinner at once. Most of us kids preferred to just sit on the big front porch while we ate dinner. We could sit and listen to grandmother tell us stories of the old days and watch the sun go down over the village. After dinner we would sit on the porch and continue the story telling or watch the night sky at the various stars and natural light. There was no electricity on the island during these years.

We knew that there was another great day coming tomorrow, and for us kids it was a great time of our lives. I could feel then that this was a great place that was becoming deeply rooted within me. I was a little older than most of the kids, but I could tell that they felt the same about their deep roots. And after all these years some of them still live on the island and the island have been home to them all their lives. Some reside at Mt. Arena right beside the banks of the Waccamaw River. As each generation come and go there have always been many that have chosen to remain on the island, even unto this day when many of them work on the mainland, they still choose to commute back and forth to the island each workday.

The Pathways to Mt. Arena

Mt. Arena is the largest Gullah settlement on the island, as this is where most of the people reside. It is not surprising that most of the residents today chose to reside at Mt. Arena because that is the location of the first settlement. Some of the kids that I played with in Annie Village reside at Mt. Arena because that is where their great, great, great grandfather and others made the first settlement on the island for the freed slaves. They know that their roots are deeply embedded on the island, especially at Mt. Arena.

I could sense this even on my short visits during the summers because my cousins that lived at Annie Village would always walk to Mt. Arena to socialize and play with the other kids there. Some days were fairly hot and I knew we were not just walking along the pathways just to see the sights along the way. Although it was a lot of fun walking the pathways and sandy roads, and sometimes cutting through the woods all the way from Annie Village to Mt. Arena.

I felt that they were not going all the way to Mt. Arena not just to visit their cousins, but because there was a deeper calling. We would visit and play and frolic around the surrounding areas of Mt. Arena all evening. It seemed like we visited every house and spoke to everyone in the settlement before we were ready to leave. We would even go down to the banks of the river to see if there was anything there, like a big gator or something. Sometimes it was almost dusk before we finally made our way back to Annie Village.

We always made it back in time to enjoy our good dinner on the front porch at the big house. The days went by quickly, and before I knew it the summer was up and it was time for me to return home in Conway to return to school. Those summer days on the island were truly wonderful and inspiring, and it seems like only yesterday even though it was over a half century ago. I knew that those good old days would not last forever.

Approaching the Dock at Mt. Arena on a
warm summer day

This is the Sandy Island Landing as it looks when you are leaving going to the Mt. Arena Boat Dock on Sandy Island

The Sandy Island School Boat leaving Mt.
Arena and crossing the Waccamaw River
to return to the Sandy Island Landing

People relaxing at Mt. Arena right beside the
banks of the Waccamaw River on a nice outing
on a summer day

This is a watercolor painting by T.J. Pyatt
of the New Bethel Baptist Church located
on Sandy Island, S.C.

Migration Away – California Living

Things were a lot different in those days, as we lived in an agricultural society in our part of the country and the pace was a lot slower. We didn't have a telephone or television at our house in Conway until the mid fifties, when we finally got a small black and white television. The early telephone was a party line, and you could only use your telephone in your house if your neighbor was not already on the party line talking, otherwise you would be hearing the other parties on the line carrying on their conversation. We had a few manual typewriters at school because this was before computers.

Industry was becoming more prevalent and beginning to boom even larger as we moved deeper into the industrial society, even though many people still made their living off the farm. The small family farms employed people in those days, and operating small farms were productive. But major progress was a-coming, although it was difficult to foresee the 21st century technological society we now live in. We knew that our generation could not live on in isolation and expect to make progress and have the type of life that a career or job in a larger city would offer.

Most of us came from large families and the small towns around the low country had limited educational and economic opportunities for us in those days. Many residents took the only opportunity available to them in the larger cities or the military. We studied hard in school knowing that there were limited opportunities for us and that we would have to migrate away.

After graduating from high school I went to California to further my education, and didn't get back to Sandy Island too often over the years. As years passed I knew that most of the older generation had died out, and that there was a new landing just beyond Brookgreen Gardens. Some of the direct descendants of the Gullah people of Sandy Island had migrated to various cities to work and live.

Migration away from the south became normal and most students looked forward to graduation from high school and moving away to work. Some students went directly to college from high school, but most didn't have the college tuition, and scholarships were rare in the late fifties and early sixties. I knew that I had to work my way through college, and that I would eventually achieve and accomplish my goals and be productive. Today I am happily retired with more leisure time to enjoy life on the island under somewhat different circumstances.

Many of my cousins that I spent my early summers with on the island also migrated away to jobs and careers. They went into many different professions, and some are teachers, military, and judges. History has recorded the success of the Gullah people of Sandy Island, and I'm grateful to have been with them at an early age, as it helped shape my philosophy and direction in life.

I didn't get to see all of them too often over the years, but my heart was always with the Gullah people of Sandy Island because I am Gullah and one of them, and looked forward to the day when I could spend more time with them. Every time I came home to visit I would make it a point to at least go to the Sandy Island

Landing to see my uncle Samuel. My uncle even though retired was still crossing the Waccamaw River each weekday to get and deliver meals to the senior citizens on the island. I was amazed at how healthy and active he was after living on the island over fourscore years.

My Gullah upbringing influenced my lifestyle while I lived in California. I was in the city to get an education and work, but I was never a part of the city. Deep down within I knew I could never be of the city because my deep Gullah roots and faith kept me focused internally in another direction, a direction based on a deep faith and belief in God, and I was determined to continue in the spirit of the Gullah people of Sandy Island. I knew there were problems in the city that could sink you deeply in the midst of chaos and confusion.

Problems of The City

I was in the city studying and working, and I was never really a city guy, and never got too caught up in the city lifestyle. I was therefore able to avoid a lot of the major problems that seemed to engulf so many of the young people who were born and raised in the cities. Many of them would walk around with their pants hanging halfway to their knees, just hanging out. After seeing so many people become victims of the snares of city life it made me even more appreciative of my Gullah upbringing.

I knew that a big part of their problem the environment that they were raised in. I knew that if they were raised in the Gullah tradition and had their deep roots growing up that they would be stronger and able to better reject the road to destruction. At a very young age we were taught that we must stay in school, study and work in order to make our life better. This is a part of our spiritual heritage and deep belief in God as passed down from our ancestors.

We know that our ancestors worked hard for us to have a better day, and now that we have more educational and economic opportunities, that we have a duty to stay in school, get a skill and be productive and successful. What better way to honor our ancestors, and keep their spirit of accomplishment alive in the good life we now have because of them. There are still many problems that remain, and we can resolve and overcome them with the proper guidance and preparedness. We need not be or remain segments of a young generation lost beyond cyberspace stuck on the bottom of the economic ladder.

Our history is full of success and accomplishments under much more adverse conditions. It pains me to know that still so many of our youths of today do not know of the history of their ancestors who were brought to these shores centuries ago. A deep knowledge of their past will better enable them to confront their situation today.

About 40% of the Blacks in America today can trace their roots back to the seaports of Charleston, S.C. where the ship captains unloaded their cargo of the residents of West Africa, who were brought here to be slaves and work the fertile lands of the low-country. Our ancestors worked hard and accomplished a great deal. We must remember their rich culture and heritage, and not get caught up in the snares of the world. As we approach the critical crossroads on our journey through uncertain times, it may become easy to get caught up in the confusion and chaos of the moment. But if we can acquire a vision we will see clearly the path and choose the right road when we arrive at those critical crossroads.

Many of the children of my generation have decided to migrate back to the south to their roots. It is not just to get away from the problems of the city, but many of us feel a deep yearning to return to our roots at the places we grew up so many decades ago. Sometimes one has to go back to his roots for a-while to fully recollect and record events that otherwise be lost forever. It may benefit generations to come if they can more easily access, and learn and know about their ancestors and culture. It will make them more productive, and therefore a better world for all of us.

Migration away from our roots decades ago gave us opportunities to get jobs and careers, and now a reverse migration will give us the opportunity to continue and finish what we couldn't in the past. Various get-togethers and reunions over the years have kept us in touch with our Gullah roots. There were mostly informal reunions in the early years, as most people who had migrated away tended to try and return home for visits during the holidays. Holidays were a time to see the former graduates who went away to further their education, and to seek jobs and careers. These were the type of informal reunions that we always looked forward to.

Reunions - Over the Years

As the years went by and more and more graduates migrated away, the numbers that returned for visits during the holidays got larger and larger. Going to church during the holidays was a good place to see former classmates who had come home to visit. There were not many other places to meet or socialize during the early years as public places were still segregated in the early sixties. There were not many places in the community that was large enough to accommodate large crowds except the churches.

Various informal reunions took place at the school, athletic events, and at houses of some family members. As years passed and the Alumni grew larger it was organized into an Alumni association. With the Alumni Association there came formal reunions with scheduled and organized activities during the holidays, especially during Christmas and New Year. Contacts and friendships were maintained and we could better communicate with each other all year from various parts of the country.

As more years passed and as more children were born to our generation, it became apparent that these children even though born in the cities should know their roots and heritage. Classmates and family members would come home bringing their children, and as the children learned about their parent's childhood home they became more eager to learn more about how their parents grew up in these small towns. They had a chance to ask their grandparents questions as all three generations were together if only for the holidays.

The grandparents could begin to see that their grandkids even though being raised in the cities had some of the character traits just as if they were raised in the south. Grandchildren became more attached to their grandparents and a deeper bond was being formed, and the grandkids wanted to spend more time with their grandparents.

Formal family reunions began to take place and organized events lasting days would be scheduled. Cars and busses full of families would come from the cities back to the low-country for these reunions. Many of the formal events were held near the Myrtle Beach area, as facilities there could accommodate the very large gatherings. Some picnics were held at Mt. Arena on Sandy Island, and it was common to see three generations of families there, sometimes you would see four generations of families there, right beside the banks of the Waccamaw River enjoying the cool breeze just as so many generations before them had done.

Even the children born and raised in the cities enjoyed getting on the big school boat at the Sandy Island Landing and riding across the Waccamaw River to get to the picnic at Mt. Arena on Sandy Island. You could just see the enthusiasm in their faces the entire boat ride, and that they were glad to be going closer to their roots. Many events were planned to teach them about their ancestors and their way of life on the island. The children and everyone looked forward to the Sandy Island Family Reunion, and know it is a return home they will not forget.

It has brought them deeper in touch with their roots, and many have been deeply inspired to become achievers and more dedicated in school. It is inspiring to see so many young children and how they react and explore the island to see and learn about their roots. The Gullah spirit of excellence lives on in another generation as passed down by their parents. They have now come home and know what it's like to have a true homecoming, as it's always good to come home. They know that everyone needs a place to call home and know that their roots are deeply embedded there.

Homecoming at Last

Every person needs a place to call home, a place they can go to forget life's current problems, a place to see old friends and renew old friendships and ways of life. Older remedies have a way of solving so called modern problems. History is full of stories about people's desire to seek a better life. Poor people all over the world have migrated to where they thought they could have a better life. I migrated out West, but most of my other classmates migrated to the Northeast. The trend then was to migrate out of the South to earn a better salary. We all looked forward to returning to our Gullah roots.

After post reconstruction the Black Afro Americans who worked on the plantations in the low country counties of South Carolina migrated up the coast and settled in other communities. One such community was the Whittemore community located in Conway about 14 miles west of Myrtle Beach. The Whittemore community was made up of many small neighborhoods, such as, The Hill, Sugar Hill, Tinker Town, Granger Town, Tin Top Alley, Spivey Alley, and many more.

The local high school was, Whittemore High School, and it was a great school with dedicated teachers. The students that went to this school were prepared well for the challenges of life. Many of the students went on to become leaders in all fields and aspects of life. Going to Whittemore was an experience we will never forget.

The Whittemore Experience – The Whittemore Alumni Association is still in existence, and has various events every year. There were many Gullah students at Whittemore. The stories of the early struggles are a source of strength and inspiration for all people who must struggle through life's treacherous journey. It shows what can happen when a people refuse to give up against all odds, the human spirit triumphs!

Whittemore built character, and some of the teachers lived a lifetime in the community. One of my teachers at Whittemore was, Earnest A. Finney Jr., he taught me Civics and I was in his homeroom. He left Whittemore to practice law and was on the South Carolina Supreme Court (Chief Justice). The first Black Afro American to hold such a position since post reconstruction. Athletics was also a major part of life in the Whittemore community, and there were many good high school athletes who never got an opportunity to take advantage of scholarships because they were not offered any. I enjoyed playing baseball in the community and played on one of the best teams of the era, the Whiz Kids.

The Whiz Kids – The Whiz Kids were a unique team, we were all teenagers and played teams older than we were. We formed our own baseball team because at this time Whittemore did not have a high school team. One day in the Spring I noticed one of the community leaders (Matthew Rhue) on the sidelines watching us practice. He kept looking for a while, and then he said you guys might be pretty good, but let me hit a little infield to you. He began to hit the ball around to the infield, and then to the outfield. We were all making the plays, and made no errors. After hitting some more, Matthew said, you guys have a team here, and I can get you some out of town games, and you guys are "Whiz Kids".

And that's how the Whiz Kids were organized in the spring of 1960. Matthew worked at the Star Furniture

Company in town, and was also a mortician. For our very first game we dressed into our uniforms in his funeral home, which was located just beyond right field. We went to out of town games riding in the back of the Star Furniture Company truck. We played against teams in various towns in the area including our archrival Georgetown, and the Dillon team had a big pitcher who could really throw a country fastball. We beat him though. As Matthew would tell the story years later, after going back to work after an out of town game, his boss called him in and asked him if he was using the company truck to transport ballplayers.

Matthew answered yes, and the boss asked him where you got the money to buy gas. Matthew said we all chipped in and helped. The boss said, don't do that, use the company's gas because what you're doing is community activity and good publicity for the company. It's amazing what can be accomplished when everyone is willing to pitch in and help. Some of the players on the Whiz Kids were; James Friday, Franklin Grice, Dennis Beaty, George Jones, Jackie Johnson, Roscoe Brooks, Thomas Pyatt, James Benning, Harold Green, and Frank McKeithan. It was such a pleasure being teammates of these guys. We had partial reunions and old timer's games over the years.

We played for the city championship in 1960 and we beat Billy McCloud's Redlegs for the championship. I left for California the following year and did not play for the Whiz Kids again. But as James Friday would tell the story about how they also played for the championship the next year and won by beating the Redlegs. Friday said they only had eight players just before game time and had to go to the tobacco fields and try to get one of their players who had to work late.

Billy McCloud was one of the best athletes Whittemore High School ever produced, but his Redlegs were no match for the Whiz Kids. All of the Whiz Kids were very good ballplayers, but many of them migrated North seeking better economic opportunities. James Friday remained in the Whittemore community and was active in playing and coaching for over three decades. I looked forward to coming home every baseball season just to play in some games just like old times, and to keep in touch with my roots.

The community was deeply religious and I went to church almost every Sunday. I loved going to Bethel AME church and listening to the Jubilee choir. The Jubilee choir never used music to accompany them; they had that old time feeling, and would pat their feet and clap their hands to make their own music. They always started singing low keyed, and then they would start to pat their feet and sing louder.

After a while they started to clap, and when it started to get really good, they would stand up and keep on singing and clapping, and you felt so good you never realized there was no music to accompany them. Sister Minnie B. Alston was the lead singer of the Jubilee choir, and she was also a cousin of mine. She was from the same place my mother was from, Plantersville in Georgetown County. There is something unique about Jubilee singers, as they seem to project a physical manifestation of the human spirit, which compels you to believe that you can succeed if only you believe you can.

Even though I grew up and went to school in the Whittemore community, it was only a half hour or so from Sandy Island. The Gullah feeling and the Gullah people were throughout the low country counties. The way of life of the community and the people were something I could never get away from. The environment I grew up in gave me confidence in myself and made me believe that I could accomplish any goal or objective that I might have.

I knew that even though I had to go away from the land I grew up on and away from Sandy Island for quite a while that I would never forget the lessons I learned on my summers on Sandy Island. I always looked forward to the day when I could return and know it was a true Homecoming at Last, and not just another short vacation. Many of the Gullah children that I spent my summers with on the island are also returning home to Sandy Island, and that makes it an even bigger Homecoming for all of us.

I never doubted that this day of a true Homecoming would come because I knew that Goals and Objectives can be obtained if one keeps a deep and abiding faith and work and take pragmatic action to ensure a process for change.

Residents Strolling at Mt. Arena Boat Dock on
the Banks of the Waccamaw River

Private Boats Docked at the Mt. Arena
Boat Dock

It's a Great Outing at Mt. Arena for The Sandy
Island Family Reunion, A Coming Back to
One's Roots

Gullah People From all Over the Country Came
Home to The Sandy Island Family Reunion

Looking Down a Sandy Road Going From Mt.
Arena to Annie Village and Georgia Hill

Approaching the Main House at Annie Village
Brings Back Memories of So Many Years Ago

Goals and Objectives

A Process for Change

1. Change can be traumatic, but we can have a pragmatic transition.

2. Many speeches and conclusions are being made, but the facts must be analyzed in an adversarial atmosphere.

3. PLAN – ORGANIZE – ACT! (POA)
   All problem-solving techniques are incorporated therein. The first step in solving a problem is to clearly define the problem. Then, carefully analyze the facts. Otherwise you will be forever wandering in the confusion and chaos of the moment.

4. You must develop and implement a pragmatic modus operandi to put plans into action and thereby receive benefits.

5. Maintain a pragmatic sense of purpose, stay focused on Goals and Objectives, take action, and pragmatic change will occur. In every bleak situation there comes a window of opportunity. Use a systematic and step-by-step approach to complete the task that at first seems overwhelming.

If we thoroughly understand the past we will understand how the present will unfold and be better prepared to be in front of the curve. Many obstacles and situations will emerge to try and detract you from your Goals and Objectives. Therefore as situations arise always consider the totality of circumstances and carefully analyze the facts. A good knowledge of one's culture and heritage is essential to achieving one's Goals and Objectives.

A Knowledge of One's Culture is Essential

A good knowledge of one's culture and heritage is essential for happiness and achievement. I learned a lot about my culture and heritage at a young age, and knew early on that my father was born and raised on one of the Sea Islands in settlements founded by former slaves during post reconstruction. I knew that they built their homes and became self sufficient by growing and producing what they needed to survive. Visiting the island was a wonderful experience every time I got to go there as I was growing up. It is still a wonderful experience to go back now to the island's various reunions and see such a wonderful foundation that gave so much to so many.

The Gullah-Geechee culture and heritage is alive and strong all up and down the low-country, from North Carolina to Florida. There are many Gullah events during the year in South Carolina. Beaufort County, S.C. is the site of various events and a Gullah stronghold for events to preserve the culture. The

Penn Center is on St. Helena Island in Beaufort County, and it was here that one of the first schools for freed slaves was established, and it is preserved today.

Gullah-Geechee people have migrated back to their roots after working and retiring from jobs and careers all over the country and world. They are very much interested in preserving their culture and heritage, and are carrying on the good traditions that they learned from their parents, and are continuing to pass it down to other generations. Some have various gifts and cultural shops, and some continue to make various artifacts, baskets, hammocks, and some continue the old ways of fishing. It's a hobby to some of us who are retired from careers, but it's a hobby that has real meaning and value. The rich history and culture of the Gullah-Geechee people is truly remarkable, especially the Gullah people on Sandy Island whom I know so well and where my roots are.

You Can Only Reap What You Have Sown

The youth of today must grow up in a highly industrial and technological society, with a tremendous amount of pressure and distractions. And without a very strong foundation they could very easily go astray. We are losing an increasingly large number of our youth to the wrong ideals. We can be forever learning, but never able to come to the knowledge of the truth. Therefore it is very imperative that we reach deep within and regenerate our rich cultural and heritage experiences and pass them along to the youth of today.

It is a continuing struggle to obtain Economic Autonomy in our communities. But my early experiences and upbringing has prepared me well to continue in the spirit of the Gullah people of Sandy Island. Be careful of the stones you throw, for you shall surely reap what you sow, and be careful how you criticize, misuse and abuse your elders. For they have suffered the indignities of iniquity, and borne their burdens in the heat of the day. Their agony is written within their faces, and they have the wisdom of the ages. Wisdom cannot be taught in classrooms, and there is no substitute for the experiences of life.

You can only reap what you have sown – If you didn't plant anything, there will be nothing for you to reap. You cannot reap where you have not sown, you cannot reap what others have sown. Many people are looking for a free ride and free benefits. But there can be no real benefits without burdens. If you did not bear the burdens of the struggle, you will not reap the benefits of the struggle.

If you did not put anything in, you will not get anything out. If you did not make a deposit into the bank, you cannot get a withdrawal from the bank. You can only reap what you have sown; there is no free salvation. All must pay their dues! Many people only show up at harvest time seeking free benefits. But they will be disappointed for they will see and know that you can only reap what you have sown. No soul can reap where it has not sown. No Burdens, No Benefits!

A New Generation on the Timeline

Sandy Island is still a unique and a truly wonderful place, in its pristine and natural setting just as it has been for centuries. But many years have passed and there is now a new generation on the timeline. Even though we all may think our generation is the best for us, and that's just normal, for as there were generations before us there will be generations after us. As of today most of the residents of Sandy Island are the 4th, 5th and 6th generation of the freed slaves that settled on Mt. Arena, and a few youngsters are of the 7th generation.

Development is not coming to Sandy Island now, so the old ways of life will not vanish completely. Now that most of the island is a preserve, it insures that most of the island will remain as it has for centuries in its natural and pristine setting. Generations come and go, but the natural beauty of the island remains unchanged as it has been for centuries.

Even with a new generation on the timeline, the customs, habits and folkways of the residents have remained intact, even as times have changed. The 21st century technological society has brought many advances and some technological changes to the island, there are some things that remain the same.

The current descendents of the Gullah people residing on Sandy Island must live without some things most people take for granted. The Gullah settlements are still isolated and are sparsely populated, and the island is not incorporated and is still isolated with no bridge to the mainland. There are no local government offices on the island and no public officials. There are no public services such as, police, fire or medical facilities, no schools, no transportation or shopping facilities. There is no mail delivery to the island and no place to get a newspaper on the island, and no garbage pick-up on the island, the island that is truly isolated.

The residents of the island must get in their motorboats and cross the Waccamaw River to go to the Sandy Island Landing at the mainland to retrieve their mail from their mailboxes. They must also take their garbage to the Sandy Island Landing to dispose of it in the dumpsters that are parked there. There are no stores at the Landing, and the nearest store from the landing is over three miles away where one can pick up a few things.

An emergency call to 911 is a call to the mainland for help that will take a while for outside help to reach the island. When a house catches on fire it will probably be a total loss, as the fire vehicles must park at the Sandy Island Landing and take motorboats across the Waccamaw River bringing fire personnel and equipment to fight the fire. There are limited responses by fireboats in certain situations, but most houses are too far inland for fireboats to be of any help. About all the firemen can do when they reach the island is to prevent the fire from spreading into a forest fire.

The residents of the island must be jack of all trades, and look out for, and protect each other, just as they have been doing for generations. Some residents are volunteer firemen, and a fire vehicle is on the island, but fire fighting equipment is limited. The residents are and have always been the first responders, and fire prevention has always been a top priority. The residents understand their responsibilities and obligations as passed down to them from prior generations, and they have always been eager to do their duty.

The Gullah people have always been very resourceful and did what was necessary to survive in this isolated environment. They have made it through some very difficult times, and it is certain that they will make it through difficult days to come, and make it through the Long Day.

Through The Long Day

The Gullah people made the best of some difficult times and their fortitude carried them through some very difficult situations. The early Gullah people had a strong and deep abiding faith and built churches on the islands to worship in. They worked and lived off the land and some were tremendous artists and sculptors. They produced some of the best rice in the world, and during post reconstruction they worked the land and became self sufficient and independent. They produced everything they needed to survive and had all types of livestock. They had smokehouses to cure their meat and they canned their own food and even had plenty left over to take to market. They empowered themselves and their communities and became independent and self sufficient amid tremendous difficulties.

They are examples of how residents of the communities now can become empowered by seizing the moment and obtain economic autonomy. My father was born and raised on Sandy Island, one of the Sea Islands. I can remember my early days visiting on the island, and how amazed I was at the independence of the people on the island. They had all they needed to survive, as it was a self-contained community, and sometimes they didn't come to the mainland for months. There were a number of residential areas on the island and I remember going to visit them all and taking in the sights of the moss trees, sand hills, and river inlets all around. Cows were strolling with bells around their necks and children playing all over the island.

Our linkage, tie and bond are strong and will carry us through the long day if we use the same fortitude that our ancestors had. The road and days ahead may be rocky at times, but with this fortitude we can meet all challenges along the way. The Gullah people brought it with them from West Africa, and passed it down to their descendants that reside on the island today. And as we move on throughout the Long Day and approach critical crossroads in our journey, we too can be certain that we will choose the right pathways in that Long Day.

The Old Main Big House at Annie Village
Brings Back Many Memories of
So Many Years Ago

Children on Sandy Island Having Fun and
Frolicking in a Sack Race

The Sandy Island Family Reunion Brings Together Gullah People From All Over the Country and World

There is Some Large Very Old Moss Trees
All over The Island

A Nice Summer Day at Mt. Arena at Picnic
Tables under the Big Old Moss Tree beside
the Waccamaw River

Residents Still Walk These Same Sandy
Roads That Have Been Walked For
Generations to Get to the Settlements
on the Island

This Feeling Within

What is it that says to you, do your thing? Is there something from within speaking? An Inner Being, a Spirit, a Soul? What motivates you to do what you know and feel is right? Does not to get it together really mean, to treat your brothers and sisters with respect? Is this not the same as repenting? What is this strong force from within? Which keeps saying do your thing and get it together. Is this everlasting feeling the part of you that can never die? Your Soul?

We have got to go back along the wayside, for too many of our brothers have strayed. Humanity has been betrayed, but not yet disinherited. To combine that which is, with that which is not, but could be is perhaps our hope. So let us all go back to the old-time way. This materialistic education will not save us, let us realize this. Let us continue to develop our minds in this society, but forever look toward the light. We are not the saviors of humanity. But we may be humanity's last chance to redeem itself. So lets' point them toward the everlasting light. We must go back to the old-time way. There is a place for us somewhere.

An educated man with no morals is one of the most dangerous creatures, to ever roam the face of this earth, for he delights in corrupting the Soul. We must go back to our true religion that had the power to move men to be Just, for to do otherwise is to perish. God did not forget man. It was man who strayed and commercialized religion. But from within our youth we shall find truth, for it is written, a child shall lead them. And time will surely bring you home. I am what I am because of the Grace of God. I am not what I am not because of the

Mercy of God. So let's walk together brothers, all the way to the Promised Land. For therein lie the foundation of youth and the tree of life. We shall see the Great Promised Land. How long? Not long, for I can feel my people getting it together.

The Gullah People have always had a
Very Deep and Abiding Faith

We may have come from humble beginnings in this sojourn or weary land. But we have made great progress and achievements, and with many achievements more to come.

We know our past has taught us the great things that we can accomplish if we remain focused and proceed in a pragmatic direction.

Going Home to Sandy Island, Home of the
Gullah People

We must keep a firm grip upon reality and not forget our history. For any people who forget or remain ignorant of their history are doomed to repeat it. Even though life at times seem dark and dreary, if you will but push on there'll be a way, and you'll find it. Let us unite with any man for a just cause, but with no man for an unjust cause.

Let us transgress not, and walk in the doctrine of Justice. For we have been touched by the hand of fate.

Some Residents Migrated Away to Get an
Education and Jobs and Careers

History is full of stories about people migrating to seek a better life for themselves and their families. The Deep South is full of such events, even from the days of post reconstruction.

Our past history of overcoming obstacles is a source of strength and inspiration for all people who must struggle through life's treacherous journey. The human Spirit triumphs when a people refuse to give up against all odds.

SANDY ISLAND - HOME OF THE GULLAH PEOPLE

From Humble Beginnings Many Generations
Have Come

Every person needs a place to call home, a place they can go to forget life's current problems, a place to see old friends and renew old friendships and ways of life. Old remedies have a way of solving so called modern problems.

True knowledge comes from a higher source. Sacrifices will lead to a freedom of the Spirit and Soul, and enable us to obtain economic autonomy.

The Sandy Island Church Boat Sits Beyond
The Sandy Island School Boat Awaiting
Residents

As the old man stood at the landing and reflected. Within this frown upon my face is the agony of the years. I stoop because upon my back I have borne my burden in the heat of the day. In the sweat of my face have I have tilled the earth. I've been out in the storm of life too long, and I'm coming in out of the wilderness now, so move on over and make a little room in that circle.

Strolling Along the Banks of the Waccamaw
River at Mt. Arena

Much was accomplished by past generations under conditions that must have seemed very bleak at times. But when things seemed dark and dreary, these great people kept their Spirits up and gave strength and courage to all those who were fortunate enough to see them reach deep within for the fortitude they needed.

They kept their light a shining, so those who followed could have an easier time.

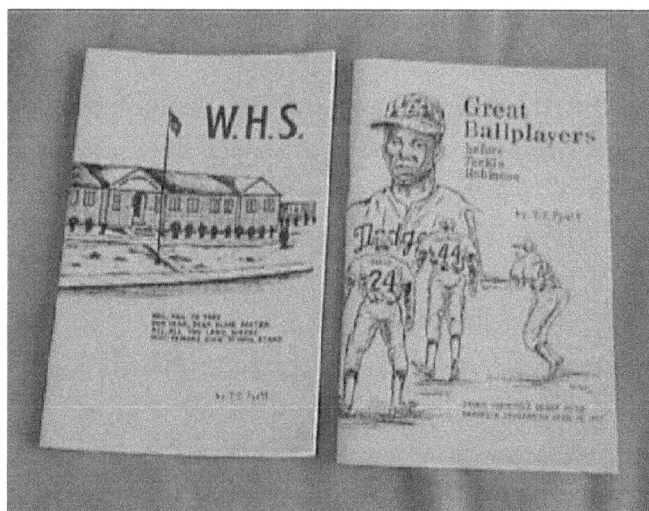

Some of the Gullah People Were Very Good
Athletes Even in the Days of Old

The many achievements of the Gullah people during post reconstruction were tremendous, and have taught us a great lesson. We should never forget their struggle for it is a beautiful part of our Heritage.

Without their sacrifices, there would have been no better days for us and we would not have been given the solid foundation on which to build a better future.

Their Legacy will live on into infinity!

The Struggle Must Continue So That the
Days Ahead Will Be Even Better For Future
Generations

Remember, history has taught us that many before us had a harder time and prevailed. If we will but keep moving on we too will succeed just as they did. This message is clear even from the beginning of History!

Only by staying in the game and staying focused on what must be done will produce any results, and Goals and Objectives accomplished.

If the prior generations could succeed under the adverse circumstances that faced them, so can we.

History Will Record the Triumphs of a
People Who Refused to Give Up and
Accomplished Much

A Renaissance

History has taught us many lessons that were a major driving force in our lives over the years. And now we have come back to our roots and are coming back to our roots in larger numbers in the years to come. We have traveled many journeys and borne our burdens over the years with the same fortitude as taught to us by our prior generations. We have carried on the spirit of the Gullah people while working full time jobs and careers for so many years. And now as more and more of us retire and come back to our roots, it gives us a great opportunity to revitalize our communities in the Gullah tradition even more. We can be a catalyst for a new renaissance and the economic revitalization of our communities and an even brighter shining example for the younger generations.

It has been said that we are entering into a new era and that this era requires new responsibilities. A new spirit of volunteerism has been called for. This is a call for good citizens to volunteer as they see fit in order to improve their communities. This new era needs a deep and sincere commitment from all citizens who want to see and commit to pragmatic change in their communities. All good citizens should have a right to feel and be safe in their communities. The community in which we live is a good place to start, for we will not be able to tell others what they should do if we do not do that which we should do for ourselves in our communities.

The call for a new spirit of volunteerism is a call for good people to pause-reflect, and listen to the choir that's deep within your conscience, and then to proceed in a pragmatic direction which will improve the community. The people who live in the community know what they need to be safe, and they must stand up and be counted if we are to see and pragmatic change in this new era. Our ancestors taught us and gave us the correct moral values that enabled us to come through many situations in the past.

This same value system will take us through obstacles on the road to progress now and in the future. A revitalization of the community is a must in this new era. We may encounter difficulties along the way, but we must remain committed to the ultimate objective, and we shall emerge victorious as long as our cause is Just (Justice). A renaissance will improve the economic status of the community and will improve the health and safety of the community. As the community obtains more economic autonomy it will enable the economy at large to be less depressed. Volunteerism can also help in the cleansing of the Soul as it enables people to give back to their communities by helping others.

This has always been a tradition in the Gullah communities as the people were forced to rely exclusively on each other in their isolated settlements. As we march into this new era we also will be going through a Long Day of Atonement, and volunteerism can be a critical part of the healing and cleansing process. And we can develop and implement a pragmatic process for change as we work together for a Just cause (Justice). It's time for all good people to walk the walk and forget those who only will talk the talk. Volunteerism may lead to economic networking within the community and with other communities throughout the land. You may find out what long lost high school classmates are doing in their communities across the country.

The Society at large must pause and reflect, and make a commitment to pragmatic change in the new era, for a new day is also dawning, a day in which greed and corruption will not be the order of the day forever, for as the new day begins to dawn we shall surely reap what we have sown. And if we end up with nothing or something we don't want, then that's what we planted with our free will. If it's growing in your garden, the assumption is that you planted it there. It's your harvest and if it's not what you expected, check out the deeds that you planted. This is a golden opportunity for us to help the young generation even more as they trek out into the world.

There will be some who will lead many down a long road to chaos and confusion and con them out of their life savings in the name of progress. Therefore it is imperative that as the Gullah retirees return to their roots that they take an active and visible role in passing on their traditions to the younger generations just coming up in this new era. For many will not know of the lifestyle and ethics that we were raised in, and they are the very one's who will benefit greatly from our experiences and struggle to become successful and productive in this society.

The young generations of today are emerging in a new and highly technological era, and need a solid and strong foundation in order not to fall for some of the snares that awaits them. If they thoroughly understand the past and their culture and heritage they will be in a much better position to remain ahead of the curve, and accomplish their Goals and Objectives. Our linkage, tie and bond are strong and are deeply rooted in the struggles our ancestors fought and became successful in spite of such obstacles.

Tranquility and Peace of Mind - is what many are seeking. But there is only one road that leads in this direction; therefore it is imperative that we seek truth and follow the straight and narrow. As we journey on through the day we will face some profound culture changes. We must face the facts as they exist today, and cannot live in the old world that we once lived in growing up in our very isolated neighborhoods and communities; otherwise we will end up in the danger zone. We have been thrust upon the front lines. Let us stand up, face the facts, seize the moment, and make the very best of the situation that confront us.

Retirement is generally a time in the life of a person that they look forward to in order to relax and enjoy a more leisure lifestyle and enjoying the good things in life. We can enjoy the good things in retirement as well as making a deep commitment to continue to pass along the traditions of the Gullah people to the young generation.

We can see changes all around us and some areas are transforming into new renaissances right before our eyes. We have a choice either to seize the moment and be a pragmatic part of change or become victims of change. Future benefits await those who are prepared for the challenges of a new day. Economic autonomy will come for those who seize the moment and are prepared to take advantage of the changing global economy. The legacy of past generations have taught us this and if we understand the past very thoroughly we will be better prepared to deal with the future as we journey through the long day. There are some experiences in life that will give us the fortitude we need to carry on.

Some people who grew up in some of the smaller communities down south have a type of ingrown fortitude that carries them through many precarious situations. I have particularly observed the life and habits, customs and folkways of the communities around the Sea Islands. The people have a knack for living off the land with a tremendous amount of fortitude and independence. They were landowners and grew most of what they needed with some to spare. Their land was passed on from generation to generation. I remember life in the Whittemore community, which was not too far from the Sea Islands. Many of the residents of the Whittemore community had their roots in the Sea Islands, and were therefore dedicated to making life better for all in their community.

Much was accomplished by working together with dignity and respect for each other and especially for the elders of the community. The children went to school and didn't create turmoil and destruction for the teachers. Everybody knew everybody and we all felt safe in walking about the neighborhood. People were vigilant and watched out for each other and for the safety of the neighborhood. Many of the young people from the Whittemore community became professionals and migrated all over the country and the world and became leaders in their communities. The success of so many young people from such a small community deep down south is truly amazing.

Growing up in such a small and isolated community gave the young people the fortitude they needed to cope with the larger communities throughout the land. The adults in these isolated communities took it upon themselves to teach the children the proper moral values and respect for their elders. It is this type of testimony and faith that I know will help lead and point the way through the straight and narrow in the new renaissance. Life in the city and smaller towns is much different today and can sometimes be filled with chaos and confusion. But even in the darkest hour there will appear a flickering of light that will point you to the straight and narrow.

There are many distractions in the city that may be tempting for so many young people, therefore it is imperative that our elders with wisdom impart a little to the younger generation so that they can be much better informed. Otherwise many will end up grown, but not fully informed and therefore not able to recognize many of the snares in disguise. Many people have different beliefs and traditions on how things should get done and even spend endless hours talking about doing good things. But without pragmatic action pursuant to a solid plan no substance is achieved. And many of the young generation may become lost and fall by the wayside for lack of pragmatic guidance.

Defined Objective – We must stand up and be committed to bringing about even more progress in the new renaissance. Our objective must be clearly defined as we march into this new era as we use our past experiences to make life in our communities better for all people.

A New Direction –The power to do this must be manifested from within. That which is manifested from within is of the Spirit and the Soul. Therefore it is from a source far greater than man, so man cannot give it to you. But men working together in unification for the good of the group can accomplish much. We must keep alert and seek new concepts and innovations from our fellow men as we past along the good traditions of the past. For to accept only one's own concepts and innovations may lead to a self imposed ignorance.

Journey By The Water's Edge

Many decades ago as we were strolling along the bank of the Waccamaw River in and around Mt. Arena on Sandy Island I knew and could feel that a new era or renaissance would come to this isolated island. I knew that one day we would be able to tell and show the world what this lifestyle is about and has produced over the generations. There is really nothing new under the sun but I knew that this day of a new revitalization would come and that we would be prepared for it by our life experiences, and would one day return to stroll along the river. I remember that day so long ago.

I took a walk down by the Riverside just to stand at the water's edge. Life is like the water's edge, and the river can be very cruel, cold and unforgiving. The river is rising and I know why the river is rising. The river's currents can be very deceptive and misleading, one moment calm and peaceful, and the next very violent and treacherous. So watch your step as you tread by the water's edge. Life in this society can also be very treacherous and uncertain, trials and tribulations may come, and obstacles placed in your way.

Ask and it shall be given to you, Seek and ye shall find, Knock and the door shall be opened so wide that no man can close it to you. For your true comfort is from a higher source, and may not come when you want it, but it's right on the timeline. Many people are yearning for peace and freedom and will fight for their liberty when their freedom is in question. But true peace and freedom are by products of JUSTICE, and lasting peace will not come until there is JUSTICE. Therefore, the tranquility and peace of mind we seek will continue to be elusive until we stop and pause and seek and march down the right road where peace and freedom resides.

And as we continue our Journey By The Water's Edge with renewed vigor, let us remember that the river is rising in the latter days.

The River is Rising

As we stroll along the bank of the river we can see far out over the horizon, and we can see that the river is moving faster now and beginning to rise and will rise even higher in these latter days. Many changes will come in this new era with a magnificent renaissance. Many that are first will fall because a New Day is dawning. A New World is coming with a New Value System. I know its coming because the River is rising higher and higher than before.

I know why the river is rising.
I know where we are on the time line.
I know when to move on up to higher ground.
I know what will happen when the river
  overflows.
I know who will be washed away.
I know how the New World is coming.

The Prophet Daniel looked and he saw the abomination of desolation standing where it ought not. I know why the river is rising, and I know that every soul must reap what it has sown.

We must be ready. Let us not keep dreaming and fall by the wayside. Action is necessary! Apathetic stupidity will keep us in the chaos and confusion that abounds all over.

Our ultimate destination must be a noble one. The journey may not be easy. Life is like a journey by the water's edge. We must be careful how and where we step or we may wade in over our heads. Life like the River can be very treacherous with many unknowns.

Therefore, it is imperative that we remain focused on the straight and narrow and proceed in a pragmatic direction, and we will accomplish our Goals and Objectives. Our ancestors gave us a solid foundation upon which to stand, and without such a solid foundation you may easily be washed away by the rising river. For every effect there is a cause.

The Law of   Cause and Effect

A New Day is Dawning – A New World is coming with a new value system. Greed and corruption will not be the order of the day forever. The new value system will not be predicated upon blind greed with the blind leading the blind. If you can open your eyes and see the facts, and carefully analyze the facts, you will understand. The new millennium will rectify many past situations, because the law of cause and effect says you will reap what you sow.

For every cause there is an effect. When you have a lingering problem, you are experiencing the effects. The effects will not go away until you deal with the cause, and properly address the cause, sometimes referred to as getting to the root cause of the problem. Many people are afraid of the future because they do not want to reap what they have sown.

The law of cause and effect shows that you must establish your own educational and economic institutions within your own neighborhoods and communities; otherwise you will never obtain economic autonomy. If we can establish great religious institutions within our communities, then we can certainly establish economic institutions within our communities. No one else can act on our behalf. Our lingering problems will not go away until we deal with the cause. This is the law of cause and effect. We must: PLAN – ORGANIZE – ACT!

Education alone does not necessarily translate into economic autonomy. We can get a good education and maintain a value system that let us live and give something back to our communities. It will be a terrible mistake to expect perpetual free benefits. You can only reap what you have sown. It will not be difficult to obtain whatever you need if you will remain focused and proceed in a pragmatic direction. Remain in affinity with a higher source. We all must take that journey by the water's edge in one way or another.

Blow Gabriel Blow

What's that I hear now, ringing in my ear?
Tis the sound of Gabriel, blow Gabriel blow.
Blow your horn man blow, blow Gabriel blow.
Let it sound so loud till it vibrates the clouds,
So profound till it wakes up the dead.
I want to be ready when it sounds,
But if death takes me to the ground,
I want to go easy Lord easy,
Cause my soul feels judgment bound.
Just tell my mother not to be shocked,
Cause I'm just going to the mountaintop.

What's that I hear now, ringing in my ear?
Tis the sound of Gabriel, blow Gabriel blow.
Blow your horn man blow, blow Gabriel blow.
Play it loud, stand tall and dark like the clouds,
Looks like Jacob's ladder there within that vision,
Souls going home with their cross of redemption.

Such ecstasy is only subsequent to the agony, pain and
strife.
Tis the only cure for a sin sick soul.
Then it shall be free to roam forever.
For within that straight and narrow is the key to that
lock,
that's why I'm judgment bound to the mountaintop.

What's that I hear now, ringing in my ear?
It's louder now and oh so near.
Coming to loose these bonds forever.
And we shall soar to majestic heights,
To the grandeur of that which is not, but shall be.

Hear that whistle, must be a train yonder coming after me,

Blow Gabriel blow, cause I'm judgment bound to the mountaintop.

The River is Rising Out in The Horizon
as We Stroll

Twilight on The Island is a Beautiful Sight;
and as this Day Ends, a New Dawn Comes

The Twilight –

As we approach the end of the long day and the sun is setting low, many have fallen by the wayside because they did not follow the straight and narrow, but tried to come in their way. And to those who have fought the good fight of faith, the victory is yours and you shall reap the benefits of your struggle. You have borne your burden in the heat of the long day, so come on in as there's room in that circle for you. You have emerged from the long day with a new mindset and pragmatic purpose, and are prepared to stand up and take action and let your light shine brightly in the world. Others will see and know that it is true that you can only reap what you have sown. It's harvest time now, so enjoy the benefits of your struggle, it's time!

Your faith and patience have brought you to this day at this special point in time. If you can have the faith of Daniel in the lion's den, the faith of Shadrach, Meshach, and Abednego in the fiery furnace, the faith of Job in his days of distress, then you like Jonah will come out from the belly of the whale and emerge anew in this great new day. This new day shall surely come as we have been foretold all things.

If no man is an island then there will come a time when he will have to leave the safety of his island and journey across the sea of uncertainty. And then he will realize that he cannot function alone and was not created to function alone. But together we can become a very formidable force, which will have to be considered.

Life is a very peculiar journey, and each man must decide in which direction he will journey. For no man can serve two masters and each man must decide whom he will serve. I know not how long, dark or difficult the night may be, but we must push on for the morning will surely come showing clearly a New Direction that will lead to a New Day with a great new renaissance.

I'll make it through the Long Day of Atonement and have no fear, for deep down within is this feeling of a unique heritage in a strange land. And when the final battle is fought and the victory is won, we shall be among the victors. We must do what must be done now for we know not for whom the bells may toll or for whom the chariot is coming. For if life is just an interim part of one's total existence, and then death is not just a tragic inevitability, but can be a pragmatic progression of life. **If there be not one among you who can fill the emptiness of the ages, then we should seek it from a higher source.**

We are a multitude of transplanted Souls; therefore it is imperative that we utilize the kind of moral reasoning that will enable us to proceed in a just and pragmatic direction.

THE ROAD TO SANDY ISLAND

However Long, Dark or Difficult the Night May
Be, There's always a Road That Leads Home

If That Road Doesn't Take You All The Way to
Your Isolated Island; Take Your Boat for That
Final Journey Home

Old Sandy Island School

From Humble Beginnings Many Have Come
And Have Kept a Deep and Abiding Faith for
Generations

May God Bless and Keep Within His Grace,
Our Precious Sandy Island Family

Sandy Island Today –
Still The Home of The Gullah People

And today after so many generations have come and gone and after so many centuries have passed which has brought tremendous changes to areas near Sandy Island, but not onto Sandy Island so as to destroy its natural environment and pristine setting. Sandy Island is still as isolated as it has been for centuries, and although many things have changed for the better, as there are more modern conveniences on the island now. Sandy Island today is still the home of the Gullah people, and their customs, habits, and folkways are still the same as passed down by their Gullah ancestors who organized the first settlement at Mt. Arena for the freed slaves during post reconstruction.

The residents of the Gullah settlements on Sandy Island today are the direct descendants of the Gullah people who were brought to these shores centuries ago. The properties were passed down from generation to generation, and many of the residents today reside on the same land that their forefathers resided on five, six, and seven generations ago. Their roots are still deeply rooted in the good traditions of their ancestors, and this is still very evident in their character, hospitality, and commitment to excellence and achievement.

Many changes have come over the years to society in general, and they have changed to some extent as the world around them changed. But it is quite obvious that they made a commitment to retain their culture and heritage during so many years of rapid and modern changes that they had to live through, on the island and all over the country as they migrated to jobs and careers.

They have adapted to the changing national and global economies and have remained competitive in the workforce. Even though still living on an isolated island many of them have worked and competed and had very successful careers in the 21st century society we now live in.

We all have to live in and compete in this 21st century technological society, and now no matter where you live you have access to the world electronically. We can communicate with each other on-line and have access to the World Wide Web and E-mail, and this is a part of our life now even on isolated Sandy Island. It is also wonderful to be able to E-mail my cousins on the island or call them on the telephone; progress has been wonderful for residents on and off the island.

The descendents of the Gullah people have done quite well all over the country and world, and as we retire we will have more time to come back to our roots on Sandy Island and enjoy the good life of the past, as the island is still isolated and in its serene and pristine setting. You can still stroll in isolation on the sandy roads all over the island, and hike through the woods and hear only the wind blowing on the leaves. The Waccamaw River has remained the same, and its banks still retains the cool breeze from across the river. The river still provides food for those who enjoy fishing in a tranquil setting.

We all yearn to come back home at some point in time, or at least attempt to. Some people ask why go home to retire, but one never needs a reason to come back home. We all have a duty to preserve our culture and heritage.

138

We will preserve our culture and heritage, and Sandy Island will always be the home of the Gullah people, as our roots are deeply implanted there. I thank God for being a descendant of the Great Gullah people.

This Generation first settled Mt. Arena

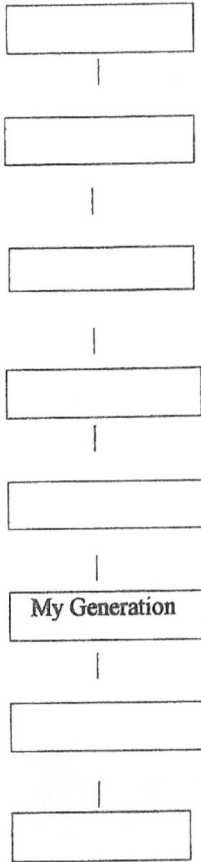

```
┌──────────────┐
│              │
└──────────────┘
        │
┌──────────────┐
│              │
└──────────────┘
        │
┌──────────────┐
│              │
└──────────────┘
        │
┌──────────────┐
│              │
└──────────────┘
        │
┌──────────────┐
│              │
└──────────────┘
        │
┌──────────────┐
│ My Generation│
└──────────────┘
        │
┌──────────────┐
│              │
└──────────────┘
        │
┌──────────────┐
│              │
└──────────────┘
```

There are a few senior citizens above my generation, but the first four generations have all died out now.

Sandy Island
Home of the Gullah People

Our Ancestors Were Hard Workers!
And Accomplished A Great Deal!
We Must Remember Our Rich
Culture and Heritage!

The Art and Insights of a Gullah Descendant

I am a direct descendant of the Gullah people who were born and raised on Sandy Island, and are of the people that organized the first Gullah settlements on the island. My father was born and raised in Annie Village on Sandy Island in large and extended families. I therefore had some very early experiences living with the Gullah people on Sandy Island during the summers, and these experiences had a very profound impact upon my life. Their way of life and independence greatly influenced me in my life as I pursued careers in art, business and writing.

The following pages contain art and insights as seen through the eyes of a Gullah descendant.

T.J. Pyatt

From the Cradle of Civilization to the Shores of
the Infinite
We Have Kept Our Light A-Shining

Secrets For Success

Acquire Economic Skills! Pray & Work
Go to School! – Stay in School!
Do For Self! – Forget About Shortcuts.
Acquire Expertise and Experience. Work Experience!

PRODUCTION:
Acquire Economic Skills!
Produce Quality Products & Services
Obtain Ownership & Control of
Economic Entities (Yours)

DISTRIBUTION:
Marketing – Advertising

CONSUMERS:
Retail
Turn Over $ Dollars in Your Community

Remain Focused on Goals and Objectives.
Use a Systematic and Step-by-Step Approach to
complete huge tasks.
Constantly Probe and Analyze – Utilize a Real
Time Action Plan.
Clearly Define the Problem and Carefully
Analyze the Facts. Don't be systematically
manipulated into economic dependency on
others outside the community. Acquire
Economic Autonomy!

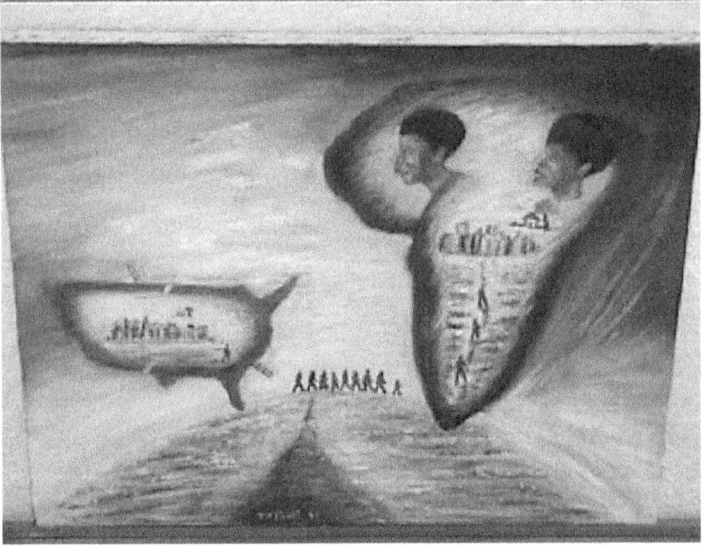

The Road to Success May Not Be Easy at Times, But Continue Your Journey and Reap a Good Harvest

PRACTICE TRUTH – TEACH TRUTH – KNOW THE TRUTH

For it is written that each of you will be rewarded according to your works.

And faith without works is dead; therefore, your works must manifest your faith. Practice Truth – Teach Truth – Know the Truth.

If you don't Practice Truth, you cannot sit with me in my booth.

Many people seeking relief from stresses of the day get caught in snares.

And are popping pills and drinking alcohol all up and down the boulevard.

Clouds of people caught in snares roaming around with their absent guard.

Playing around and finger popping at juke joints, up and down the boulevard.

Young people in pain hooked on mind twisters, living a life so very hard.

Popping pills in the Devil's Den, they've dealt themselves a terrible card.

Beware; it is a surety, that according to your works you shall be rewarded.

Work is essential, for you can only reap what you have sown.

Seeds on good ground will triumph and you'll see what you have grown.

So till your land, and you will surely have a good harvest in your yard.

And won't feel the pain of those on mind twisters; down on the boulevard.

And accelerate going back down to a quick return to the dust of the ground.
Partying won't do, for according to your works you shall be rewarded.

Our works must be based on truth to avoid the pitfalls on the boulevard.
So Practice Truth – Teach Truth – Know the Truth! You are seed on good ground.

There's a terrible storm full of pain all up and down the boulevard.
People caught up on mind twisters, tears raining, pushing them down.
The Devil's in his Den with his snares, keeping them down on the ground.
If they don't rise up soon, they'll quickly return to the dust of the ground.
So stand up where you are, make it better, and you'll receive a good card.
And see clearly as the light brightens the way, for within you is your guard.
And your guard within will brighten the way and you'll see very clearly, and avoid the snares in the Devil's Den all up and down the boulevard.

I judge not any man, but it is written that if any would not work, neither should he eat. Therefore, if you don't practice truth you cannot sit with me in my booth. For you will be rewarded according to your works and reap what you have sown.

Practice Truth – Teach Truth – Know The Truth!

For you shall reap what you have sown.

THE DRAGON'S POISON BOWS

Who sold the Dragon the poisons for his arrows in his bows?

Don't they know they shall reap exactly what they sow?

The Dragon disguised, as a lamb is really a beast.

And he comes to attempt to destroy the true wedding feast.

His arrows are filled with poison sold to him by those who should know.

That it is a surety that they will reap exactly what they sow.

But they that know the Truth cannot and will not be deceived.

For the Dragon comes first; and many wanderers will believe.

So Practice Truth – Teach Truth – and Know The Truth!

And you won't end up with the dreadful Dragon in your booth.

For you shall be rewarded according to your works,

And reap what you have sown.

Long, dark and cloudy days may come with many woes.

The Dragon's inventory filled with poisons by those who stooped so low.

But they should know that they will surely reap what they sow.
The light will shine on those who manifest their faith by their works.
And each and every one rewarded according to their works.
Double minded men walking around with their blind eyes wide open.
Their actions producing victims and fallout victims from their drug tokens.

Sorcerer's addictions creating more victims and fallout victims.
Mothers having to raise their grandchildren as their children become hooked.
Their valuables stolen by addicts before they are caught and booked.

Who sold the Dragon the poisons for his arrows in his bows?
Double-minded men dancing with the Dragon, don't they know?
That they will get stuck with the poison arrows in his bow.

They should have known that they shall reap what they sow.
The Dragon's wagon filled with poison inventory piled so high.
Supplied by double minded men who cheat and lie.
Dancing with the Dragon and are available for hire.
Double minded men dancing in the Dragon's den and the den's on fire.

Children are Crying and Youngsters are Dying

Children are crying and youngsters are dying in the
danger zone.
In their city village is a danger zone, but it's their only
home.
They come into the world, born into the danger zone.
They grow up in the danger zone, with nowhere else to
roam.
Trouble abounds all over and they're left to mourn in the
terrible danger zone.
Life in the danger zone leaves them weary and worn.
Amid poverty with no phone to call for help in the
danger zone.
With all hope gone in that zone, but it's their only home.
Clouds of hopeless children and youngsters in that
terrible danger zone.
Amid mind twisters as they roam in that danger zone.
Mind twisters on many corners within sight of their
home.
Children crying and youngsters dying as they roam in
that terrible danger zone.

Street memorials on too many corners in the danger
zone.
Victims lying prone by others who claim it's their turf
home.
Multiple generations falling victims to handouts in the
terrible danger zone.
In poverty they mourn, and roam, until their days are
gone.

Many on handouts trapped in the terrible danger zone.
Men forced to leave home so their children can get
handouts in that terrible danger zone.

Handout policies producing more broken homes, and
broken homes producing children that mourns in the
danger zone.
They roam all over that zone, for it's their only home.
But when they roam too far, they become victims lying
prone.
Mothers left to wail, children crying and youngsters
dying in that terrible danger zone.
Mothers left to mourn in that terrible danger zone.
Youngsters that roam become victims lying prone when
sirens sound in that danger zone, and mothers are left to
mourn.

Handout policies excluding fathers from their children's
home in the danger zone, contributes to no hope in that
zone.
So sirens sound and mothers mourn, and children keep
crying and youngsters dying in the terrible danger zone.
Some may run seeking a safer place; seeing what has
been grown.

Stand up where you are and make it better, and safe to
roam.
Beyond the dark and cloudy days, a harvest in the
morning.
For we all must reap what we have sown,
and bells may toll beyond that terrible danger zone.

Listen, Listen to the Choir That's Deep Down
Within Take Heed and March On

March On Toward the Straight and
Narrow and Don't Stray
There is a Light There Guiding You

Demons are Hibernating in Drugs and Alcohol

As chaos and confusion abound from coast to coast, some people seek refuge in drugs and alcohol. But this is a mirage or fool's gold, and a tunnel into self-destruction. Anything that destroys the mind is not a relief; it is a trick or snare by Satan himself. But you have power over the demon and must command him to get behind you and stay there. Some people try to run away from situations or find temporary relief in vices.

But remember that the big demon Satan himself hibernates in drugs and alcohol, and if you put too much drugs and alcohol in your system, the demons come out of hibernating, and awakes to do great damage to your mind and body to get you to destroy yourself. Don't put a hibernating demon into your body, for he will take advantage of you in your weakest moment, for he delights in your destruction. So remember don't get caught or suspended in the stupor of slumber.

To not get caught in the stupor of slumber throughout the long day it is imperative not to overindulge in alcohol and popping pills in the Devil's Den. For only those who remain alert will be able to see clearly and act appropriately when the critical crossroads appear, as we all have to walk that Long Day of Atonement.

Keep your head up high and march on and accomplish your Goals and Objectives, a new renaissance awaits you.

154

The Gullah People Have Always Had a Very
Deep and Abiding Faith That Kept Them

They Have Always Organized Religious
Institutions In Their Communities

Their Faith Have Given Them the Strength to
March On Throughout The Years

The Acquisition of Economic Skills

Acquiring Economic Skills is a prerequisite to obtaining
Economic Autonomy.
Symbolism and clichés will not triumph over substance
and give you benefits.
Go back to school, stay in school and acquire the needed
economic skills.
Such skills will enable you to climb rugged hills and
cure many untold ills.
Don't get mislead, sidetracked or tricked by the folly of
a fool.
For the acquisition of economic skills will only come if
you stay in school.
It's really not cool to just party, play ball and hang
around shooting pool.
You'll end up on the bottom stool just like any other
junked used tool.
The ownership and control of economic entities are for
those who stay in school.
For they will be able to avoid mind twisting pills and
pay their bills.
The ownership and control of economic entities requires
economic skills.

If you don't stay in school, you'll easily fall for the folly
of fools and fail.
And end up just another number on the books in jail
with no bail.
And for some, sirens will sound for victims lying prone,
as mother's wail.

Caught in the danger zone, hooked on mind twisting
poison pills.

And now back to the dust of the ground lying still with no will.

And the cycle continues for another generation seeking the same short cuts.

For without economic skills they'll end up in the danger zone in the same huts.

Economic skills will enable you to avoid many of the illiterate ills that kill.

And give you sufficient resources to pay your bills and leave plenty by will.

Stand up and face the reality of the moment, and don't be left standing at the dock.

With no chance of going on that beautiful trip with those who stayed in school.

That's why they have economic autonomy and not stranded with the wrong flock.

So go to school and stay in school and acquire economic skills!

That's how you get to be first and a true number one.

The young ones' must listen to their elders who have walked under the sun.

Mind twisting pills will lead to the wrong road and lead to the Dragon's Den.

And you'll end up all alone in some wretched out of the way prison pen.

Symbolism and clichés will never triumph over substance.

And after you get through with all the symbols of success.

You will still be on the bottom of the economic ladder and must confess.

That to obtain economic autonomy you must acquire economic skills.

For to continue with the folly of fools will give you many untold ills.
So go to school and stay in school and acquire economic skills.
Then you can truly be number one and will have reached the highest hill.
Without economic skills you'll remain on the bottom of the economic ladder.
And others will look at you and continue on and on in silent laughter.
Go to school and stay in school and acquire economic skills.
And you won't have to worry about getting illiterate ills.

BE PREPARED TO COMPETE
IN THE GLOBAL ECONOMIC ARENA
(And Stay Prepared)

**The Global Economic Arena is now before us and
The Economic Playing Field has been dictated to us.
We must be prepared to Compete in it!**

- Identify Potential Job Opportunities (categories) in the Global Economy.
- Identify Economic Skills needed in the Global Economy.
- Acquire Economic Skills (not just degrees) needed in the Global Economy. (Identify your strengths and weaknesses – Reason for leaving last job?)
- Establish Priorities and engage in Economic Networking. (Have Long Term Economic Goals). Avoid that which is Contrary to Sound Doctrine.
- Obtain and Maintain the Proper **A.C.E.** (Attitude – Conduct - Environment).
  > **A**ttitude -Must be conducive to Accomplishments.
  > **C**onduct -Don't Engage in Conduct Detrimental to Progress.
  > **E**nvironment – Avoid Negative Influences and Bad Associations.

Being computer literate is essential for learning and may help you stay ahead of the curve. You can do research online and keep up with the latest technology and financial markets. Information is online. Maintain an up to date resume. You may even have to e-mail your resume.

In every economy in the world there is a need for good financial record keepers, accounting and bookkeeping. Other skills are also needed and in demand, such as, paralegals, medical assistants, auto mechanics, electricians, plumbers, sales, etc.

The economy may be down now with high unemployment, and companies are not hiring. There are many skilled and management people looking for work. Some are even going back to college and making it harder for some first time students to get accepted into college. Colleges and Universities all over the land are receiving more applications than they can accept. Many are becoming discouraged and dropping out of the job market. Different Economic Skills are now needed in the Global Economy.

Don't give up, know who you are, stay committed and prepared. Continue to send out resumes and continue to update and upgrade your Economic Skills. You may take classes at night or online. So be prepared as you may end up starting your own company or business. Continue to turn over dollars in your community as this will help create jobs. Be prepared for your opportunity because in the darkest arena a flickering of light will shine showing you your opportunity. Be Prepared!

Many of us Gullah Children Also Attended the
Old Whittemore High School in Conway

JACKIE ROBINSON'S DEBUT WITH
BROOKLYN DODGERS ON APRIL 15, 1947

You Must Stay in the Game and Compete With
Everything You've Got, and You'll Prevail

Practice Financial Accountability

Financial Accountability is imperative for one's financial well-being, and should be based on a Pragmatic Economic Agenda. One must acquire the necessary economic skills (not just degrees) to obtain economic autonomy.

Economic Autonomy – To include the ownership and control of economic entities within your community. Have Long Term Goals that will enable you to become independent and self sufficient.

Economic Agenda – Determine what must be done and do what must be done for you to obtain economic independence! Establish Priorities and Act. Identify major problems that need to be resolved.

Financial Accountability – Be prudent and establish checks and balances, internal controls, to ensure your continued financial good health. Make sure that your Revenues are always greater than your Expenses. Monitor your Debits and Credits, and use T-Accounts if necessary. We must operate prudently in this 21st century electronic banking system that gives us easy access to ATM's and all types of credit and credit cards, as it is so easy to become overloaded with debt nowadays. Debt is the destruction of many.

Analyze financial statements, income statement and balance sheet, and make sure that the balance sheet is not overloaded. Make sure that your current assets to current liabilities ratio is sufficient. Avoid non-productive people and freeloaders.

Remember, you will retain no benefits without accepting and living up to your responsibilities and obligations!

Month _____

Income   **Expenses**

Make sure that your income is greater than your expenses, and your expenses should include your necessaries. To continue to spend more than you make leads to debt and major problems.

Month _____

Income	**Expenses**
	Mortgage-Rent
	Insurance
	Taxes
	Electricity
	Heat
	Water
	Garbage
	Telephone
	Cable TV
	Clothes
	Miscellaneous
	Emergency

Make sure that you have identified all you monthly bills, and also budget for other bills that are not due monthly but will have to be paid within the year, such as taxes and insurance. And you may have enough left for a vacation if you keep your credit card debt down and under control.

167

The Island is a Peaceful and Tranquil Place as
One Roams Its Sandy Roads Passing Old
Houses Filled With History

Sunset on Sandy Island

As The Sun Sets at Mt. Arena on Sandy Island
it's an Amazing Sight Even Though I've Seen
it's Setting Over The Waccamaw River for Over
Six Decades

That is a view of life on and off the island for over a half century as seen through the eyes of a Gullah descendant. We now have the further opportunity to continue on and share our experiences and make the world a better place because of our efforts to make life and living better for all we have had the opportunity to come in contact with.

Any society that does not collectively proceed in a righteous direction will eventually end up in a precarious quagmire. Our life's work should be a living legacy to all those who knew us as we journeyed on our sojourn here among them.

May God Bless and Keep Within His Grace, Our Precious Sandy Island Family.

Art Director – T.J. Pyatt
www.tjpyatt.com

Index